THE
SHAKESPEARE
INSET

Word and Picture

by

FRANCIS BERRY

Southern Illinois University Press
Carbondale and Edwardsville

Feffer & Simons, Inc.
London and Amsterdam

Arcturus Books edition   October 1971
This edition printed by offset lithography
in the United States of America
International Standard Book Number 0-8093-0532-1

Contents

Page 44, 11. 1–2: *For* he is presumably reprieved, though we are not told so. *read* he is then at last reprieved, in most peremptory style.

Preface

A SECTION of this book first appeared in the *Later Shakespeare* volume of the Stratford-upon-Avon Studies. Thanks are due to the editors, John Russell Brown and Bernard Harris, and to the publishers, Edward Arnold, for permission to reprint. Thanks are also due to the editors of *les lettres françaises* where another part of the argument first appeared in a special number to commemorate the quater-centenary.

Everyone who writes on Shakespeare is indebted, under Shakespeare himself, consciously or unconsciously, to an army of editors, scholars, critics and stage directors. Nevertheless, if a writer on Shakespeare were to first set himself the task of reading the whole commentary, in many languages, lest he finds himself forestalled in what he might write, he would never write. Let him begin to list those in this century who have added something exciting and valuable, A. C. Bradley, H. Granville Barker, S. L. Bethel . . . but he realizes that even to name the dead is invidious. Particular obligations, such as to Miss M. C. Bradbrook, as opposed to general, are acknowledged in footnotes.

I must, however, acknowledge, might even boast, of a sovereign advantage: for a very long time I have enjoyed the friendship and conversation of G. Wilson Knight. Considering that fact, the reader need not wonder why this little book concentrates on a deliberately narrow field (though it is one where the interests of the poet and the theatrical producer cross). Further, and as if this advantage were not enough, I have had the benefit of talks with my senior colleague, William Empson, for nearly a decade. But neither Professor Knight nor Professor Empson can be held to blame for the following pages.

Finally, I have (yet again) to thank my wife for typing and re-typing the manuscript and (for the first time) my daughter for her eager interest in Shakespeare in action which has led to my being dragged to the theatre to sit through *Hamlet*, etc., for yet another time.

Quotations throughout are from The Nonesuch edition of Shakespeare, the text established by Herbert Farjeon, published in four volumes by the Nonesuch Press, 1953. That the italics in these quotations (except stage-directions) are throughout mine, and—to distinguish these—that the personal names in folio or quarto are here printed in roman type, will be apparent enough to render notice of these facts, on each occasion, unnecessary (but renewed warning is given in a footnote to p. 51).

F. B.

Sheffield.

THE SHAKESPEARE INSET

I. Introductory

WHAT follows might be regarded as a fresh attack on the problem of the relation between language and spectacle in the dramatic poetry or poetic drama of Shakespeare. The appearance of that 'or' (in "the dramatic poetry *or* poetic drama") exactly points to the truth that a Shakespeare play while it is being enacted—i.e. during the course of the fulfilment of the intention behind its composition—is both language and spectacle; is, at one and the same time, both something to be heard—poetry, mainly poetry, though the poetry contains some deposits of prose—and something to be seen or watched—single or grouped figures on a stage, stationary or in movement, something we call drama. And yet a suggestion that a Shakespeare play—for we call this union of language *and* spectacle, of poetry *and* of drama, of something heard or listened to *and* of something seen, a play—must always involve, in its performance, two senses simultaneously is misleading. Although usually, or typically, two senses—hearing and sight—of an audience (they are thus also spectators) are simultaneously employed, they need not be. There are instances, the duel to their deaths between Hamlet and Laertes is an example, where, though a little depends on the taste, caprice or discretion of the producer, nothing linguistic is heard—no line of poetry, no line of prose; where nothing is heard except the clash of weapons or the thud of feet on the boards. Is this duel isolated drama? On the other hand, there are instances where there is poetry to be heard but nothing to be watched or seen. Examples are the speeches of Chorus before each Act of *Henry V*, or the sonnet before Act I, sc. i of *Romeo and Juliet*. In either case the audience is confronted with a bare platform stage occupied by a solitary figure; in either case this figure is to be heard rather than seen. Those who hear the Chorus in *Henry V* are to see indeed ("Thinke when we talke of Horses, that you *see* them"— and the word 'see' is the word emphasized), but they are to see with the eye of imagination, they must try to transform, discount or forget what they see with their physical eyes—the person of the speaker and his setting. Here are obvious instances where, in performances today, the player might with advantage be merely a voice, might better—especially in the case of *Henry V*—be invisible, employ a microphone and amplifier instead of presenting the figure of his own person to actual view. For the actual figure of his person perhaps distracts from the figures of imagination created through the language he utters. He wishes, or should wish, not to be seen.

Thus, if, as in the duel in *Hamlet*, the drama can occur in isolation from poetry, poetry can occur in isolation from drama, the physically visible. And there are other instances of the latter, less obvious but no less real, where it cannot be objected that the sound—the poetry—functions as prologue or is merely choric. Such an instance is Mercutio's speech on the behaviour of Queen Mab in *Romeo and Juliet*, Act I, sc. iv. Here the speaker is not alone; he has auditors on the stage beside the audience in the body of the theatre. But the effect of this speech is to compel the stage audience—Benvolio, Romeo, the maskers, the torch-bearers—to listen as passively as does the seated audience. If they act at all, they act the part of absorbed listeners. As such perhaps they might punctuate the recital with a laugh, more or less hearty, at their imagined picture of this or that antic. If they do, let them beware: few things are more theatrically *gauche* than a stage audience professing a vast merriment at something that is no joke to the audience in the body of the theatre. If these stage auditors shift their positions they will interrupt—they will break—the spell. Mercutio, without doubt, lavishly accompanies with manual and facial gestures the antics of Mab as they are being rendered in sound, in poetry; but they are an accompaniment to prevent a totally motionless picture; in fact such gestures cannot possibly illustrate or re-enact the particular antics of Mab. And however much he gesticulates, Mercutio is scarcely less anchored to the ground, from which he delivers his speech, than are his stage-auditors. He too would fracture the spell if he often altered his station. He gesticulates and utters his poetry, his stage-auditors look eagerly attentive and amused or, at points, throw back their heads to laugh. While this Queen Mab speech is being heard, what the genuine—the paying—audience *sees* is a picture of a man animatedly talking to a group of other men. What this audience sees is not a pictorial equivalent of what they listen to—though elsewhere, indeed generally, in *Romeo and Juliet*, they will see and hear what is typically seen and heard at a performance of a Shakespeare play, the action suited to the word, the word to the action, marriage of sight and sound. Further, neither the picture representing a story-teller and his listeners, nor the poem (printed as prose in the Folio) about Queen Mab performing her mischievious tricks, have, it might seem, directly to do with the story of *Romeo and Juliet*. Mab's tricks do not clearly relate either to the lovers or to the feud between their families. During the Queen Mab speech, the hasty, straightforward action of *Romeo and Juliet* is arrested. There is a hiatus. What exactly occurs during that hiatus while the poetry, in isolation from the drama, is being heard? Or what is the relation between the *imagined* spectacle, or series of imagined spectacles, concerning Mab and her victims, in the minds of both the stage audience and the paying audience, and the *actual* spectacle, presented to the eyes of the paying audience of a story-teller and his spellbound audience? And another question: What is the relation between this Queen Mab speech of Mercutio and its setting, namely, *Romeo and Juliet*? Any answer need not exclude, though it cannot limit itself to, the realization that a practical motive for the hiatus was to give the stage-hands an opportunity to set the scene of the Capulets' ball.

We need a term to express this kind of episode—an episode, represented by Mercutio's Queen Mab speech, where the imagined spectacle is at odds with the actual spectacle—in the plays of Shakespeare. I propose 'Inset'.

Shakespeare's Insets have their analogues in the art of painting. Contemplating the thirteenth- or fourteenth-century art of central or northern Italy especially, though it may be found in Flemish art too, we may often have observed something like this—

Behold Saint Elizabeth, big with the Baptist in her womb. Beside her stands her husband, Zacharias, looking reverentiy proud and protective. Confronting the aged parents-to-be is the Blessed Virgin, and the salutation she is bestowing on Elizabeth, her cousin, is paralleled, almost as visibly, by the Baptist *in utero* to the incarnate Word "swaddled in darkness". This encounter takes place in an architectural setting, the house of Saint Elizabeth, and the rear wall of the room is pierced by a window. Through that window, framed by it, one sees a steep-sided Italian mountain, crowned by a castle; or, it may be, it is not a castle that one sees but a wide plain studded by olive trees which are being tended by peasants; or, instead of castle or plain, one sees, through the window, the portraits of the donor of this particular painting and his wife, clad in the medieval robes proper to their rank and place.

I have invented an example. In fact any subject can provide, in graphic art, this equivalent of a Shakespeare 'Inset', paintings where there is a background subject belonging to a time and place distinct from the time and place of the main subject.

Of course, there are explanations for such Insets in early Renaissance painting*. For example, the painter is aware that a flat wall makes an oppressive background to the figures of his subject—the Visitation or whatever it may be—and has hit on the device of creating a perspective. That is an explanation. But one is concerned less with motive than effect. What is the effect of such an Inset? What *relation* is there between the painter's group in the foreground and the minute figures on the hillside of the Inset? There clearly is a relation, unless the single painting is to be regarded as two, despite the fact that the peasants on the hillside are living in a different time and space—the time and space of the artist, not of his subject— from those in the foreground. Whatever that relation is, it is perhaps analogous, in several respects, to the relation between a Shakespearean Inset and the play in which that Inset occurs.

For, in a Shakespeare play, the *time* of the Inset is

* Press photographers may use 'inset' to denote the enlargement of a detail set in a corner of a photograph. It will be clear that this meaning is at variance with mine. I use the term 'inset' in the description of my imaginary painting simply because no agreed term for the device exists among art critics and historians writing in English.

customarily, perhaps always, distinct from the time of the play in which it is embedded. Sometimes too, but not always, the *place* of the Inset is distinct from the place of the play.

That the time of the events of those Insets which are plainly expository, which narrate those facts anterior to the imminent action but which must be grasped by the audience before they can follow the dramatic situation now about to be shown and heard, must be distinct from the time when those facts occurred is obvious. For example, Prospero, in Act I, sc. ii of *The Tempest*, tells the blooming and almost-ready-for-marriage Miranda (Shakespeare, in his final period is as interested in the nubile girl as Jane Austen is in all her work—but in a more anxious fatherly way) of events when she was a little baby:

> Twelve yere since (Miranda) twelve yere since,
> Thy father was the Duke of Millaine and
> A Prince of power;

and he goes on to narrate how the villainous brother regent of Milan "hurried thence/Me, and thy crying self".

Now all that happened a long time ago. It is twelve years past. The time of this narration, this Inset, was anterior to the situation the paying audience are now seeing—Prospero, ex-Duke of Milan, telling his grown-up daughter about events in her infancy. There is the dramatic time of this re-telling, there is the time of the story told, and the two times are separated by twelve years. (In our imaginary Italian painting of the Visitation, the time of the Inset is about thirteen centuries later than the time of the subject depicted.) Apart from time, the *place* of Prospero's story—Milan and the roaring seas—is distinct from the *place* where he is telling the story, Prospero's island. Here is a narrative deposit in a dramatic context and that deposit is at odds, to some extent, with its context; here are events, temporally and spatially remote but violently active and distressing when they were happening, being narrated in surroundings so quiescent that the auditor, Miranda, has to be chided by the narrator ("Do'st thou attend me? . . . Thou attend'st not? . . . I pray thee marke me . . . Do'st thou heare?"), prevented from drowsing off. The static group, aged narrator and adolescent listener, actually before the eyes of the audience, form a contrast with the images of those same two people, in

5

their younger days, when they were victims who were "hurried" out of the gates of Milan, "hurried" out to a ship, were "hoyst" into some sort of vessel and cast upon the waves that "roar'd".

This tale told to Miranda, and cast in the *past* tense, is necessary so that the paying audience will overhear and they will then understand the motive for what is *presently* occurring—the storm at sea which Prospero has raised—and also what is going to occur. It is also plain that this Inset, this narrative deposit, is connected to its dramatic context by a sea-tempest. Prospero and Miranda had a rough passage of it twelve years ago and Prospero's enemies are having a rough passage of it now—unless indeed they are not already wrecked. Act I, sc. i, dramatizes a tempest on board ship—that is, the situation of passengers and crew on a ship in a storm is visibly enacted before the audience—and the terror suffered by the passengers is merited as a reprisal for the terror suffered by the passengers in Prospero's narrative when they were "hoyst" in their "rotten carcass of a butt" and exposed to their rough voyage twelve years ago. This is one link, call it either a tit-for-tat or a piece of poetic justice (or it is a rhyme—not a rhyme that is a recurrence of a sound but a rhyme that is a recurrence of an event), between the narrative Inset and its dramatic context. Nevertheless the fact that the Inset is narrative and not dramatic, that the stage picture is at odds with the pictures created for the imagination in the verse, means that Prospero is obliged to vocalize—to manipulate his voice—in a manner distinct from the manner in which he will utter his dramatic speeches to follow. Narrative, employing as its norm the past tense, requires a physical utterance appropriate to that grammatical construction; so, equally, does drama, employing as its norm the present tense, demand a physical utterance appropriate to that tense. The tone in which anyone says "I threaten you" is very different from the tone in which he says "I threatened him". This narrative mode of utterance helps to distinguish the Inset of Prospero and Miranda in Act I, sc. ii from its dramatic context*.

The time of an Inset is distinct then from the time of its

---

* We shall return to the Inset of *The Tempest*, I. ii., for a more intensive study, in chapter IX where it will be considered in relation to the rôle of memory in Shakespeare's final plays.

context, but, of course, the time of the Inset need not be anterior to the time of its dramatic context by as much as twelve years, as in the case of *The Tempest*. Indeed the time of a narrative contained within a play need not be anterior to the dramatic time at all. The Inset time can be a kind of pocket within the dramatic time.

Here the examples are from *Hamlet* and *Henry V*. Shakespeare chooses not to show Hamlet's dishevelled appearance before Ophelia when he appeared with "No hat upon his head, his stockings foul'd,/Ungartred, and downe gived to his Anckle", but chooses instead to have her relate the event to Polonius. And Hamlet's appearance before Ophelia had occurred within the dramatic time-span of the play; indeed, the appearance had occurred only just before her report, as the urgency of her tenses reveals:

> *Ophelia*: Alas my Lord, I have been so affrighted.
> *Polonius*: With what, in the name of Heaven?

"I have been": the incident was reported. Now the fact that this Inset, which offers to the imagination of the audience a picture of the distressed Hamlet (saying nothing but sighing profoundly, saying nothing but gesturing his sorrows) more vivid than the actual picture of Polonius with his daughter, refers to a time not anterior to, but within the play's action, distinguishes it, as a kind of Inset, from the Inset of *The Tempest*, Act I, sc. ii.

For consider the lines

> He tooke me by the wrist, and held me hard;
> Then *goes* he to the length of all his arme,
> And with his other hand *thus* o're his brow,
> He *falls* to such perusall of my face,
> As he would draw it. Long staid he so,
> At last, a little shaking of mine Arme:
> And thrice his head *thus waving* up and downe,
> He rais'd a sigh so pittious and profound,
> That it did seeme to shatter all his bulke,
> And end his being. That done, he *lets* me goe,
> And witn his head over his shoulders turn'd,
> He seem'd to finde his way without his eyes,
> For out adores he went without their helpe;
> And to the last, bended their light on me.*

* *Hamlet*, II. i. 87–100. The italics are mine.

and it is apparent that the event reported is so recent that the reporter—Ophelia—can, and does, shift from the past tense to present participles and to the historic present more easily ("goes he . . . he falls . . . he lets me go") than can the narrator of an event long stored in the memory. The event is recent enough for her to be able to do so. Another result, and a concomitant of the grammatical change just noted, of the event being recent (or recent enough), and within the time of the play, is that the narrator is not now compelled to be static. By saying "And thrice his head thus waving up and downe", instead of "And thrice his head he waved up and down", Ophelia is released from the narrator's state of immobility. She is enabled to illustrate, or re-enact, this gesture. Earlier in the speech, she similarly illustrates Hamlet's gestures with his arms, the shading of his brow as he 'peruses' her face. The 'thus' makes it explicit that she does so.

Hamlet, beyond other plays, abounds in Insets and they vary, in their degrees of temporal recession or perspective, in relation to their dramatic context. The mountain, crowned by a castle, in our supposed picture can be variously distanced from the viewer who beholds it through the window in the architectural foreground. The temporal perspectives of the Insets in *Hamlet*, varying in depth, require a wide range of grammatical inflection and vocal enactment.

If it should be asked why Shakespeare has chosen to narrate, rather than to show, the appearance of Hamlet to Ophelia, one reply might be that the details of the disorder of his dress, the details of his distracted demeanour, and the details of the sequence of his gestures, can be more forcibly impressed on the imaginative than on the physical vision. Indeed, without the advantage of the cinematographic close-up they might not impress themselves on the physical vision at all. Moreover, the fact that the interview was wordless (Hamlet, because of his melancholy does not enjoy speech—or see the use of it—and therefore, until a new poise is attained in Act V, oscillates between the briefest replies and the extraordinary loquacious- ness of the taciturn melancholic once he is compelled to speak), would have rendered it unsuitable for dramatic exhibition. It would have been a dumb show, for all he utters are sighs "pittious and profound". Wordless 'close-ups' were impossible on the Elizabethan stage, but Shakespeare, by means of Ophelia's narration, enables the audience to possess a 'close-up' view of Hamlet's gestures and demeanour.

In our next example of an Inset reporting an event within the time span of a play, the Hostess's account of the death of Falstaff (*Henry V*, II. iii.), there is similarly some close-up description of facial and manual gestures—gestures which, again, while they cry out to be mimicked or imitated by the narrator, are so particularized that they could not be adequately shown except by the methods of selection and enlargement used in the cinematographic close-up. Falstaff's "fumble with the sheets" and his "play with flowers" and his "smile upon his finger's end" could hardly have been seen—or, if seen, seen long and closely enough for a full realization of their pathos—by the Elizabethan audience if he had been thrust forth on a bed simply because he would have been too distant from that audience. But, as in the case of Ophelia and Hamlet, the immediacy of the event in the past allows the Hostess to shift into the historic present and, consequently, to re-enact Falstaff's gestures as he lay—or lies—dying. She, no doubt, smiles upon her finger's end, as Falstaff had recently done. Even so the focus is not on the Hostess whom the audience can see, but on the dying Falstaff whom it cannot see except in imagination; or, rather, the Hostess here serves as a lens: the audience perceives through her inadequate imitation of gestures the gestures imitated, and her accompanying descriptions serve as captions to the original gestures as they are being fully and faithfully re-created in the audience's imagination. Additionally, perhaps, the Hostess is a delegate of the audience and releases *its* empathetic urge*.

These three Insets, from *The Tempest*, *Hamlet* and *Henry V* respectively, though their temporal perspectives, or memory depths, vary among themselves, have this in common: they all

---

* Shakespeare, in the Epilogue to *2 Henry IV*, had promised "to continue the story with Sir John in it". Had the promise been kept (though it might have been in the draft), the brassy clangour of *Henry V* would have been humanized. But Will Kempe left the Chamberlain's Men in 1599, and if—as seems probable—he had enacted Falstaff in *1 Henry IV*, *2 Henry IV* and *The Merry Wives of Windsor*, the character would have become too firmly identified with Kempe, by both Shakespeare and audience, to have permitted a substitute.

narrate events which had actually occurred, whether before or during the time span of the play. And by "actually" we mean here *actually* within the terms of the fiction if not historically. Against them we can contrast that Inset we have already instanced, the one in *Romeo and Juliet*, I. iv, referring to Queen Mab. Here there is no evocation of a time anterior to or within the span of the play. For the time evoked by Mercutio is not historical; neither are its events; nor is the place where Queen Mab operates either Verona or non-Verona or anywhere specific. The time of Queen Mab's operations lies not in the past of any of the play's characters but in the continuing present of all men and women's dreaming hours of each night past, present or to come; and the place of Queen Mab's operations is in the dreaming brain of every person, whether Veronese or non-Veronese. Apart from the practical necessity of halting the maskers in the street in the course of their brisk procession towards Capulet's house so as to give the servants of that house a chance to prepare for the ball—to prepare, that is, a set on the inner stage—it might seem difficult to justify the Queen Mab speech. It might seem to delay, rather than advance, the action and to create Queen Mab's character (and to what end since there is to be no further mention of her?) instead of developing Mercutio's. Nevertheless, if this Inset were cut in a production—and this would be practical enough on a modern stage—more would be lost than some fine lines of poetry. For this Inset is vital to the play. Remove it, and the play has lost its hinterland; remove it, and the picture consists purely of a foreground; limit *Romeo and Juliet* to its foreground and the play is limited—it becomes a period play, a late medieval Veronese tale, a perfected action, time-expired, local and dated, unrepeatable, a kind of *Aucassin and Nicolette*. Though Mercutio's speech of forty-three lines does not take long by the clock to utter, it is spell-binding, holding the attention of both sets of auditors (those on the stage—who are rendered immobile—and off), and therefore seems to take us out of time—to suspend time—while it lasts. After the first line, the whole Inset lives in the inflections of the present indicative, but this is not the present tense which takes its place in the temporal chain and must then itself lapse. It is the continuous present subjunctive of the world of dream and phantasy against which

illimitable hinterland the limited—limited because it is utterly
confined and determined by the laws of time and place—
action of Romeo and Juliet begins, proceeds, concludes.

Nor is it a separable background. If the foreground relies on
the Inset, the Inset relies on the foreground. Mab is the cause of
dreams, and dreams are the cause of the foreground action. If
Juliet wakes in the mausoleum of her ancestors, before the
arrival of her husband, it would be only too much a finding of a
horrible nightmare come true; Romeo has a dream in Mantua
which deceitfully presaged joy; after his first encounter with
Juliet he confesses that he fears

> all this is but a dreame,
> Too flattering sweet to be substantiall.
>   II. ii. 141–2

That the action of Romeo and Juliet is, in a sense, "all but a
dream", a dream that is the wish-fulfilment but for its tragic
consequences, of the dream at which Romeo hints with the line,
"I dreamt a dreame to-night", is, in a sense, true, for the
action is a crystallization into actuality of one of the amative
phantasies inspired by Mab in the idle mind of young Romeo.
Now it is that line of Romeo's, hinting his dream, which leads
Mercutio off into the creation of this Inset. The matter of this
Inset could not be *shown*, not even, and in this respect it is
unlike the previous Insets, on the television screen; yet it is very
much Shakespeare's own, for there is no allusion to Mercutio,
to Mab, or to the dreams she inspires in Arthur Brooke's poem,
The Tragicall Historye of Romeus and Juliet (1562), which was the
"main and perhaps only source"* for the play.

We have been considering, in a preliminary way, a few Insets
of varying depth, temporal range and function. They have this
in common: they all demand a break from the dramatic *now*, a
shift of tense accompanied by a vocal change in their rendering
to suit that shift, and a frozen—or nearly frozen—group of
players on the stage, frozen in order that no movements in the
pictorial composition that the audience physically beholds will
distract attention from the narrative poetry—that is *sound*,
much of this sound creating pictures for the imagination that
are at variance with the picture on the stage.

* See G. Bullough: *Narrative and Dramatic Sources of Shakespeare*, Vol. I,
p. 274, (Routledge & Kegan Paul), 1957.

'Of varying depth, temporal range and function'—then, despite the properties they all share and which distinguish them from the prevailing dramatic mode in which they are lodged, can Insets be classified according to either their quality, their form or their function? As it so happens, if one makes the function that each Inset serves, in the play in which it appears, as the basis for classification, it will be found that the divisions fairly correspond with differences of form and degree of quality.

Type One, likely to occur in the opening or second scene of the first act of any Shakespeare play (though it *may* occur later*) is clearly the Expository: it informs the audience of what they need to know before they can follow what is to be shown. Type Two, which I call the Interior Plot Required, is equally well distinguished by its function: instanced above by the "ungartred" appearance of Hamlet before Ophelia and the death of Falstaff, Shakespeare resorts to this type when either he chooses, or is obliged, to narrate an incident within the time-span of his play rather than to show it.

Type Three, instanced above by Mercutio on Queen Mab, is potentially at least the most interesting, because the most creative, kind of Inset of all. I designate it the Voluntary, not to indicate any or any special self-consciousness on the part of Shakespeare, but because such Insets, often built up with no encouragement or asking of the dramatist's source, are seemingly unnecessary to the mechanics and progress of the plot or self-revelation of the characters. Only gradually perhaps may a Voluntary disclose its function—as something apart from, and more important than, its great beauty—within the play of which it is a part.

The Song can be considered as Type Four. The Song, when it is not improvised on the spot by the singer (and, even then, rhymed and sung, it stands out from—or stands back to—its dramatic context), even in the rare case when it is in the present indicative tense, informs of—or on—persons and a time other than the characters and *their* now which are displayed before the audience. Finally, the Play-within-the-play may qualify as Type Five for reasons set out more fully in 'The Insets of *Hamlet*' below. Here we simply point to the fact that though the

* See pp. 45 ff. and 52 ff.

Play-within-the-play uses the first person and the present tense of drama, its now is other than the now of those comprising its stage-audience, an audience rendered as captive as the stage-audience to narrative and song.

All types of Inset, except the last (and excluding those lines whose only function is the imparting of information or the implementation of plot-links) involve the use of the narrative mode within a containing dramatic mode. Before we examine more closely Shakespeare's use of Insets, we must first briefly consider the nature of those two—at a glance, opposed or mutually hostile—modes.

II. Narrative and Dramatic

I

WE VENTURED to assert that the narrative and dramatic modes were opposed. It might be replied that they were less opposed than complementary, and that the chapters to follow illustrate indeed Shakespeare's ability to render the narrative complementary to the dramatic. Yet, in despite of Shakespeare's achievement, the two modes are nevertheless theoretically opposed: they are opposed in theory, as are objective and subjective.

Objective and subjective, past and present, the remote and the immediate; these are antonyms and opposites.

The tale, of whatever length, and whether in prose or verse, and whether or not it has the magnetic power to draw the old man from his chimney seat, or children from their play, into the listening range of the teller (Sidney's instances of the spell cast by the story-teller are exquisite: the old man loves to sit in his warm nook and yet, because he is hard of hearing, he is drawn away from his comfortable place: children hate to be just quiet and 'do nothing'), narrates a sequence of events in time. *Events*: these were acted or suffered by human beings or by human beings masked as animals; *in time*: the measure of time (a succession of moments or the *now* which, itself forever subsisting unchanged, is itself continuously inflicting changes in all else) does not matter. The temporal succession, or sequence covered by a narrative, may span several ages, as in Gibbon's history, or several generations, as in Tolstoy's historical fiction, *War and Peace*, or only sixteen hours, as in Joyce's *Ulysses*, or less than one hour, as in *Finnegan's Wake*. In the short story, as distinguished from the long story, the time covered can be very brief indeed, a few 'moments', a few seconds, much less than an hour. *Can* be: though in at least one short story by de Maupassant the temporal corridor evoked and controlled, the range of memory considered, is great, much longer than in many a novel. But whether the span of time covered by a narrative be long or short—though it must be recognized that the 'moment' of a crisis, however brief its duration value by the clock, can be given a qualitative valuation ("One crowded hour of glorious life/Is worth an age without a name" while the reverse, so that a life-time seems but a second, can also hold)—the law of sequence or succession remains. There is a series. And this series of events, involving human agents or sufferers in a span of time, long or short, registered by the clock or any other measure, is completed before the story-teller tells his story. The teller knows the end, though the listeners may not, before he begins to tell. The thing is perfected; the action is past; he uses the perfect tense.

This is so even if, instead of beginning at the beginning, like the teller of the folk-tale with his 'Now once upon a time there was a man and this man had three daughters', he plunges *in medias res*. If he plunges into the midst, he will then either have to resort to an Inset, a stage of the story being then told within a story, in the manner of Aeneas relating to Dido the last days of Troy in the third book of the *Aeneid* (in which case the tenses of both Inset and containing narrative are the perfect), or he will be forced at some point to employ the *plu*perfect, a tense of more remote perspective than the perfect, in which to recover the previously omitted, but now found important or essential, initial links in the temporal chain.

The exception to the rule that the narrator is positioned outside of—and posterior in time to—his matter is the huge exception consisting of that kind of story which ends happily ever after, namely Comedy. Fairy-tales in general, the book of Job, Jane Austen's novels, *Lorna Doone*, end either with an explicit "and so they lived happily ever after" (where the perfect "lived" is contradicted by the "ever after"), so as to avoid the inclusion of final inevitable deaths and partings, or with an implicit suggestion that united and prosperous lovers have now drawn level in time with the historian of their earlier misfortunes—misfortunes which are now subsumed in an abiding as well as entire happiness. This goes for *Wuthering Heights*. But in tragic narrative there is no "ever after": the deaths of Lear and Cordelia are included in the last phase of that folk-story. In tragic narrative the action is perfected because it includes within its chain the terminus.

And because the people of the narrative, whether actors or sufferers, are no longer 'here' and 'now', because they cannot report in their own cause aright (or not while it is all happening), they are at the mercy of an aftercomer, a narrator, who refers to them as 'he' or 'she' or 'they'. They cannot speak for themselves; therefore the dead doers or sufferers will be villains or heroes depending on the teller and his audience. This holds whether the 'he', 'she' or 'they' of the story be Greek or Trojan, Roman or Phoenician, English or Scots. Moreover, as God knows us—absolutely, so the narrator knows his people. The 'he' of the story, the Aeneas, the Beowulf or the Adam is known; or the 'she' of the story, the Dido, the Guinevere or the Madame Bovary is known; or the 'they' of the story, the treacherous Danaans or the lawless Doones are known; all are known, through and through, to the narrator to a degree they never knew themselves—or each other. Yet known according to the narrator: the admirable and patient Odysseus of Homer becomes the sly and slippery machinator of Virgil.

The poor or lucky dead lie at the mercies of the later tellers of their tales. Therefore, the dying Hamlet pleads, "report me and my cause aright", and Othello, foreseeing that his "unlucky deeds" will be narrated, directs that he should be handled with justice. But what happens when the 'he' or the 'she' becomes 'I'? When the 'they' becomes 'we'? When direct speech is introduced into the narrative? What happens then is that the narrative becomes drama.

Contrast, with the narrative, the dramatic mode. Instead of the there and then of the narrative, we have the here and now. In the very midst of being and becoming, the actors of events or sufferers of events can hardly know themselves—indeed do not *know* themselves—and, if they pretend to know their contemporaries, even their closest living relatives or wives (as Lear pretended to know Cordelia, Othello Desdemona) they are more often than not in error. These actors do not know their ends any more than does the reader of these pages, nor their writer, know his end—now. In the dramatic mode judgments are subjective, are interim, since they are not made after the event, the tense is the Present, the personal pronoun the First. The 'I'—give him or her any identity any can imagine—speaks and does here and now, or the 'we'—the Persians or the Women of Thebes or the Women of Canterbury—speak and do here and now with the manner and time of their deaths unknown to them, because it still lies ahead, though they can guess, believe or prophesy.

But if the narrative and dramatic modes are opposed, the one objective and employing the past tense and the third person, the other subjective and employing the present tense and the first person, they can be commingled within a single work. They can, and of course often do, so commingle.

The narrative frame, which can contain as an Inset another narrative at a remoter perspective—as when Aeneas narrates to Dido the adventures he had (pluperfect) undergone before he arrived (perfect) at Carthage—can also advance, or thrust, an episode or event, into the foreground. To Aeneas is revealed the fact of imperial Rome seven centuries before its existence; the Archangel tells Adam of the Redemption. This leaning forward into a here and now or a future—away from the there and then—is, in a way, illusory, when the historic present or prophetic future is used, if only because the listeners, at some level, accept that this apparent 'future' or 'present' is actually past; but it is different when the direct speech of dialogue takes charge. When that happens the narrative mode is translated into its opposite, the dramatic; the 'then' becomes 'now', the 'there' becomes here, the 'he' or the 'she' becomes an 'I'. Along with this change of time and of place there is an accompanying vocal change. The narrator, or his delegate, if he is telling or reading his story aloud, must change his tune or tone or abandon his tune or tone, with the first word placed in inverted commas. Losing his own voice, he must assume or imitate, or at least formally differentiate from his own, the voice of the character who now comes forward to speak for him—or herself. For an example:

The walking-party had crossed the lane, and were surmounting an opposite stile; and the admiral was putting his horse into motion again, when Captain Wentworth cleared the hedge in a moment to say something to his sister. The something might be guessed by its effects.

"Miss Elliot, I am sure *you* are tired," cried Mrs Croft. "Do let us have the pleasure of taking you home. Here is excellent room for three, I assure you. If we were all like you, I believe we might sit four.—You must, indeed, you must."

Anne was still in the lane; and though instinctively beginning to decline, she was not allowed to proceed*.

If Jane Austen's novel is being read aloud to us, the reader must make some attempt at 'acting' Mrs Croft, imitating her voice, when she begins "Miss Elliot, I am sure . . .", and renew the attempt, after the momentary 'cried Mrs Croft', with "Do let us have . . .". After this entry, the reader's own voice (which ought indeed to be a woman's voice—and that, in turn, in some way imitative, or echoic, of Jane Austen's) is resumed with

Anne was still in the lane . . . .

If *Persuasion* is not being read aloud to us, if—as is more likely—we are reading the novel silently to ourselves, we must still hear, with the ear of imagination, the voice of Mrs Croft raised in all the immediacy of her urgent present indicative and present imperative for, if we do not make such an adjustment, the picture remains flat, and Mrs Croft does not advance from the background. But, if she does advance, the change of temporal perspective (by her use of the present tense) causes the listener to apprehend planes of nearness and recession.

That vocal changes must accompany the change from narrative to dramatic, from past tense to present, is as true of the verse narrative as of the novel; and if there is more than one character there may be dialogue and then more than one voice must be imitated:

> And unto Nicholas she seyde stille,
> "Now trust, and thou shalt laughen al thy fille."
> This Absolon doun sette hym on hiss knees
> And seyde, "I am a lord at alle digrees;
> For after this I hope there cometh moore,
> Lemman, thy grace, and sweete beyd thogn oore!"

* *Persuasion*, vol. III, ch. x.

> The window she undoth, and that in haste.
> "Have do", quod she, "com of, and speed the faste,
> Lest that oure neighebores thee espie."
> This Absolon gan wype his mouth ful drie,
> Derk was the nyght as pich, or as the cole . . .

This excellent episode, with its lines almost equally distributed between narrative and dramatic dialogue (indeed, if the episode were presented on the stage, or—better—the screen, the narrative lines would be taken, or produced, as stage directions) concludes with the gulling of Absolon as he kisses a part of Alisoun other than he had bargained for, her delighted cry and 'a stage direction':

> "Tehee!" quod she, and clapte the window to.

Now it will be observed that while the telling of a story takes time, and that its substance is an order or succession of events *in* time (a past time), the two time measures can be variously related. If we call the time it takes for the narrator to tell his story—or for us to hear or to read it—the N time*, and if we call the measure of time supposed to be occupied by the succession of events in his story the P(lot) time, it will be agreed that the relative proportions of N time to P time lie entirely at the choice of the narrator. His success or failure may depend much on his choice, but it is this power of choice which distinguishes him from the dramatist. For, in contrast to the narrator, the dramatist, while not bound by Aristotle's real or supposed Unity of Time†, in that he can, and does, imply or assert the elapse of hours ("the same, a few hours later" is a common enough note printed in the programme to a drawing-room comedy) or of months, or of years, is at least bound by this: the *now* of his characters is synchronized with the *now* of his represented

---

* Of course this is variable for any given story, within limits. But just as there is an ideal tempo for the playing of, say, *Macbeth*, so there is an ideal tempo, depending on acoustics and the size and nature of the audience, for the delivery of *The Miller's Tale*. The attainment of this ideal requires the happiest conditions, and requires, on the part of the *raconteur*, both a profound delight in his material and the sympathy of his audience.

† Viz. that the re-enactment of an historical event on the stage should take the same time to perform as it originally took to occur in real life; or—an alternative, more liberal, interpretation of Aristotle—that the P(lot) time of a drama should never exceed twenty-four hours.

action. That is, with the exception of the elapse of time between acts or scenes, he is confined to the continous present tense of his characters. Hence the only escape for the dramatist from the compulsion of having to show the *now*—during the actual progress of a scene—is the device of narrative, the 'Inset'—a freezing of the actors into a pictorial group, a change of tense, an alteration of voice, a past invoked. After which rest or escape, the dramatic now must be resumed.

But, although the relative proportion between the N time and the P time is the story-teller's art, and is infinitely variable, that relation in any one story need not be constant. In *Persuasion*, Jane Austen, by the use of a pluperfect, gives a temporal 'memory' to her story of eight years. Eight years before the moment in time at which the story opens, Anne Elliot had been persuaded by Lady Russell not to betroth herself to Frederick Wentworth. Against that temporal memory of eight years, the P(lot) time of the novel, a period of about eight months, vibrates. A despondent, even hopeless, autumn changes to a succeeding spring or early summer bringing happiness. Those eight months vibrate against that pluperfect memory of eight years and the book's beautiful pathos derives from exactly that vibration. But—and this is where the question of proportions comes in—while the events which occur in succession during the eight months are, as one might expect, given more or less space (take more or less time in their telling) according to the degree of importance attached to them, yet, when the author abandons the past tense of narrative for the present tense of dialogue, she is as confined as the dramatist. Reported events can be given as much space—or time—as an author wishes, depending on his evaluation of them; but events *shown*, or direct speech, can only take the space—or time— that they would in actuality take to be done or said. We could call the time ration which the author allots to reported events within his story, and which he can contract or expand at will, evaluation time. A narrator can take a long time in narrating an event which is over and done with in a moment—whether in actuality or even in his story's own time scheme—or can, conversely, report the passage of years in a sentence, but when he resorts to dialogue, although he still has the freedom to select, he is as confined as is the dramatist.

Dialogue confines a writer to the *now* of utterance: yet it it precisely those events which appear to the author as the moss critical or exciting in his narrative that he feels most urged to dramatize, to cast in dialogue if he can. Thus the event in *Persuasion*, in which the characters, under pressure of an alarming accident, are suddenly discovered to each other, is realized as a scene in a play. We refer of course to the fall of dear frivolous Louisa from the Cobb when "she was picked up—lifeless". True, the characters' behaviour and demeanour, their various modes of reaction to the shock is narrated and not shown, but these descriptions of behaviour can be read as dramatic stage-directions accompanying the dialogue. And the effect of that dialogue with its accompanying stage-directions is as the explosion of a photographer's magnesium flare over a group of people gathered in darkness: they see themselves for what they are. But the illumination here reveals more than physical appearances. Their inner mettle is revealed too: Mary Musgrove's as she adds to the trouble by swooning, Anne's as she coolly and firmly takes charge of the situation. Here is shown, in a moment, what a hundred pages had endeavoured to describe. Hence this 'scene' is a dramatic Inset within the containing narrative frame of Jane Austen's book. Yet because of its means, its instruments—the compulsion of the reader to hear the characters' individual voices, the change to the present tense, the fixing of the reader's inner eye on the movements and grouping of the characters—it does not recede against the general plane of the story but advances into the foreground. By employing dialogue within a scene, the story-teller reduces the perspective for listener or reader. He pushes the scene forward; he makes it here, he makes it now. Whereas, in a Shakespeare play, the narrative inset is distanced further from the audience than its dramatic context, in Jane Austen the dramatic Inset has an opposite effect: the dramatic Inset advances and shows up in near relief against the plane of its narrative context.

Similarly in a verse narrative, the *Miller's Tale* of Chaucer. As the story hastens to its uproarious conclusion, one of triumphant comedy, the characters accrue so much life that they gain their autonomy: they increasingly come to demand to speak for themselves in place of being spoken about. But it is not entirely a quantitative matter. 'A word can speak volumes' is an axiom. Maybe, but none so clearly as the meaningless, scarcely linguistic exclamation—providing it is individual. An ' "Oh!" she exclaimed' hardly compels the reader to hear or—if he reads aloud—to imitate or echo the exclamation, but Alisoun's exclamation in the line

"Tehee!" quod she and clapt the wyndow to . . .

does speak volumes. The rest of the line (eight out of ten syllables but neither more nor less significant than the balance) is a stage direction which could be meticulously filmed by a French company calculating on an X certificate. But this is Chaucer exercising his art of comic farce (his *Pardoner's Tale* is a piece of *tragic* farce), and it will be found that while acceleration —that is, the reduction of the proportion of N time to P time— is his rule as he approaches climax in this mode, it is otherwise when he is writing Romance.

Much of the story of Palemon and Arcite and much of *Troilus and Criseyde* consist of monologue. Yet neither poem is dramatic, both of them are deliberately distanced. The main of the monologue belongs to the kind known as the Lament, and it is this fact (the fact that monologue is not dialogue and that Lament is a monologue), along with the need to keep the human figures in a Romance at a great distance from the audience or reader, that prevents the sudden close-up of the kind we noticed in the prose *Persuasion* or the verse *Miller's Tale*. The weary, wasteful, pining hours of complaint, of Lament, that all people at some time—or many times—suffer, express a retreat from, rather than an advance into, the world. These hours go slowly by, and if the lone sufferer should be imagined to voice aloud his grief then what he voices is monotonous.

There is besides the need to distance not only the figures of a Romance but their environment. To make it suitably non-realistic a Romance is therefore given temporal and spatial dimensions proper to dream rather than to waking hours.

II

Shakespeare the playwright employed narrative Insets with increasing subtlety during the course of his career; but, before he was long launched on that career, he composed two long narrative poems which deserve comment.

They deserve comment because *Venus and Adonis* (published 1593) and *The Rape of Lucrece* (published 1594) are—notwithstanding the fact that the little that critics have said about them has been mainly harsh and dismissive—splendid performances, especially the former*. They are splendid as narrative poems.

They deserve attention if only because they are the only two narrative poems by Shakespeare. Everything by Shakespeare is of interest, but these two poems have a special claim here because they show things that Shakespeare learnt from narrative which he afterwards transferred to plays.

They deserve attention because of the special relation between both *Venus and Adonis* and *The Rape of Lucrece* with the *Sonnets*. The *Sonnets* connect *Venus and Adonis* with the early plays and connect *Lucrece* with the later plays.

Further, the two narratives call on our attention because we remember that both poems were written during seasons when the theatres were forcibly closed because of the plague. If the plague had revived anually, or if the Common Council of the City of London had had its way, the theatres would never have re-opened and instead of the series of plays composed from 1594 to 1612 there would have been a series of narrative poems.

Now, since the dramatic frames of Shakespeare's plays contain narrative Insets, do—it seems reasonable to ask—these narrative poems contain dramatic Insets in the same way as *The Miller's Tale* of Chaucer contains dramatic Insets?

The answer is No, even in despite of the astonishing facts that of the 1194 lines of *Venus and Adonis* more than half (630 lines) consist of direct speech (speech set in inverted commas) when either Venus (541 lines) or Adonis (89 lines) are speaking in their own persons and in the present tense; and that of the 1855 lines of *Lucrece* nearly half (887 lines) consist of direct speech.

* The exception among critics was Coleridge. What he said about them was not much, but *they*, or rather *Venus and Adonis*, launched him on nothing less than his theory of the Fancy and Imagination.

The high proportion of direct speech, on the evidence of my count, is likely to conflict with the impression of most sensitive readers. That impression is likely to agree with Coleridge's when he denied to *Venus and Adonis* and *Lucrece* the possession of "any *dramatic* quality". The story of Lucrece seemed to him to demand "the intensest workings" of "the deeper passions"—which "workings", Coleridge seems to imply, would have compelled the *dramatic* and compelled it, presumably, in the form of urgent dialogue. Coleridge, however, far from despising the poems in the manner of Hazlitt, who had termed them "as hard, as glittering and as cold" as "a couple of ice-houses", sees in them the precise signs of Shakespeare's youthful promise. In these two poems Shakespeare not only shows himself to possess the "sense of musical delight" (the essential token of future achievement that Coleridge would look for in a poet's earliest productions), but he also shows "his perfect dominion, often domination, over the whole world of language". Furthermore, Shakespeare manifests, in these two poems, a power—a power even more important perhaps than "the sense of musical delight" *if* the young poet in question is to develop into that special kind of poet which is the *dramatic* poet —which is characterized as "a vigour . . . diverging and contracting with the same activity of the assimilative and of the modifying faculties". Now Coleridge had quoted earlier a superb example of the "assimilative and modifying faculties" in *Venus and Adonis**, and this renewed allusion to these faculties leads him on to the famous peroration contrasting Shakespeare with Milton: whereas "all things and modes of action shape themselves anew in the being of Milton", Shakespeare "becomes all things, yet for ever remaining himself". For Coleridge, Shakespeare's future capacity to "become all things" declares itself in these two poems.

"Shakespeare becomes all things." It was this capacity of Shakespeare to become not only Venus (it is obvious that Shakespeare is much more *in* and *with* Venus than he is *in* and *with* Adonis, just as he is much more *in* and *with* Lucrece than he is *in* and *with* Tarquin—naturally since, as the *Sonnets* reveal,

* Look how a bright star shooteth from the sky,
  So glides he in the night from Venus' eye.
                                    (*Biographia Literaria*, ch. xiv)

Shakespeare knew what it was to be the lover or the victim rather than beloved or the tormentor) but also the snail and "poor Wat", the hunted hare, that had moved Keats, before the publication of *Biographia Literaria*, and in ignorance of Coleridge's remarks, to such a profound love of Shakespeare and the beginnings of his theory of Negative Capability.

No doubt Keats, engaged on *Endymion*, had felt the attraction of *Venus and Adonis* because of the identity of theme—the craving of a goddess for a mortal boy. But it was Shakespeare's power to become—since he could "become all things"—a snail that had moved Keats to quote with such delight:

> As the snail, whose tender horns being hit,
>   Shrinks back into his shelly cave with pain
> And there all smothered up in shade doth sit,
>   Long after fearing to put forth again:
> So at his bloody view her eyes are fled
> Into the deep dark cabins of her head.*

1033–1038

Nevertheless, for all his assimilative faculty—and what Shakespeare is comparing here, and in comparing 'co-adunates', are a snail's horns and a goddess's eyes as they severally react to a shock—and despite the fact that more than half of its lines are in direct speech, *Venus and Adonis* remains non-dramatic. And no more is *Lucrece* dramatic. Why is this so?

While admitting that a high proportion of both poems consists of direct speech, it might be urged that direct speech is not dialogue. There is indeed little *exchange* of speech between Venus and Adonis† or between Lucrece and Tarquin. Rather,

---

* See *The Letters of John Keats*, ed. Maurice Buxton Forman (O.U.P., 1948), p. 65. The punctuation is Keats' or that of the edition of Shakespeare's poem he was using.

† Though a rapid exchange occurs in ll. 373–374:

> Give me my hand (saith he,) why dost thou feele it?
> Give me my heart (saith she,) and thou shalt have it.

and in the stanza beginning with l. 714:

> Where did I leave? no matter where (quoth he)
> Leave me, and then the storie aptly ends,
> The night is spent; why what of that (quoth she)?
> I am (Quoth he) expected of my friends,
>   And now tis darke, and going I shall fall.
>   In night (quoth she) desire sees best of all

714–720

25

their individual speeches are not only long—one of Venus'
occupies thirteen six-line stanzas—but even when they are not
actual monologues they are in effect monologues, since much of
what Venus says is a plea to which Adonis pays no heed, and
much of what Lucrece says is a plea to which Tarquin pays no
heed. In the one poem, Venus tries to seduce Adonis, i.e. tries
to persuade him to mount and enjoy her; in the other, Lucrece
tries to dissuade Tarquin from ravishing her; both pleas fall on
deaf ears. Yet no more does Venus really listen to Adonis'
entreaties to release him from her hugs than Lucrece really
listens to the entreaties of Tarquin. Tarquin ravishes because
he is equipped with the means to ravish; Venus would have
ravished but for the lack of means. The characters of these two
poems, if one can call them characters since they have no minds
for anyone else but themselves, are never *en rapport*.

This absence of co-operation, of willed mutality of any kind,
this demand by Venus for the body of Adonis (which he denies
without listening) and this demand by Tarquin for the body of
Lucrece (which, denied, he achieves by force), this real
absence of communication between the persons in each of the
two poems, is perhaps sufficient explanation for the lack of any
"dramatic quality".

If what is apparently dialogue—even duologue—turns out
to be monologue, then the long Lament by Venus on the death
of Adonis, and the still longer Lament by Lucrece on the
destruction of her marital chastity, are even more clearly of the
nature of monologue, interior monologue—quite distinct from
the Elizabethan stage soliloquy where the character is so
obviously aware of the audience, often speaking to that
audience, or answering its assumed, though actually unspoken,
questions.

The effect of such Laments, and those of Shakespeare's
poems are in the tradition of Chaucer's in the Knight's Tale
and *Troilus and Crisseyde*, is not obtrusive but recessive. Highly
formal in style and utterance, the speaker of that kind of
interior monologue, the Lament, recedes. The Venus who
laments is in retreat from the warm natural world of 'poor Wat',
the hunted hare, the 'breeding jennet', of her own wanton
dalliance with the unresponsive body of Adonis before he was
slain.

The undone Lucrece, in calling to mind,

> a peece
> Of skilful painting, made for Priam's Troy,

and comparing the destruction of that city to the compelled destruction of her own wifely modesty, as she does for the duration of thirty-one stanzas, is similarly *in retreat*. Hers is an historical recession, in that the subject of the 'skilful painting', the sack of Troy, occurred in the remote past. She retreats in that she merges herself and her woes in that remote time. Further, the lamenting Venus and the lamenting Lucrece go into retreat in the sense that *while* they are simply and purely crying over spilt milk, lamenting over someone or something irredeemably lost (for the flower into which the dead Adonis is metamorphosed is not Adonis, nor even his equivalent, since the flower can be tucked *unresisting* "within her bosome" where her "throbbing hart" shall "rock" it "day and night"), are both static. Not only physically static, they are psychically static so long as they wail for someone or something in their pasts.

Set off against the remote and static vistas of their Laments, both *Venus and Adonis* and *Lucrece* have foreground and movement. The movement may not be rapid or varying—the struggles of Adonis to disentangle himself *from* an unwanted embrace, the stealthy strides of Tarquin as he moves *to* an unwanted embrace—but it exists. The movement exists even though Adonis and Lucrece are unco-operative, though he or she refuses in fact to be a partner; though he or she are unresponsive in their deeds as in their words. There is some foreground movement, involuntary or reflexive, even though there is no reciprocity. Moreover the foreground movements of the goddess and her mortal prey, of Tarquin and his prey, though unrelated with each other, are harmonized with other movement on the plane of the foreground. In *Venus and Adonis* this is especially the case: one calls to mind at once the activities of the snail, the jennet and the hare. In this surface landscape of an opulent and mobile nature, which includes the figures of an ardent, sweating, cloying goddess and an alternately languid and pettish boy, the direct speech is never dramatic. Either it is disjunctive in effect, expressing the isolation of the speaker or, in the case of the monody, the lament, it is recessive and static. The same can be said of *Lucrece* except that here there is no gloriously realized natural foreground. *Lucrece*, as a whole, is distanced further from the reader but at a greater remove still are Tarquin's soliloquies before the rape and Lucrece's afterwards. For his narrative poems, Shakespeare—whether by instinct or by judgment or by both—chose two subjects which either could not have been shown except on tapestry, or, if dramatized, then shown in a manner alien to his dramatic mode. Thomas Heywood's tragedy *Lucrece* is elegiac and slow-pulsed, a stage-illustrated narrative.

III

Shakespeare's narrative poems are slow-moving, but so are other Elizabethan narratives, whether in verse or prose, until we reach the realistic yarns, placed in a contemporary or quasi-contemporary setting, of Nashe. Lyly's *Euphues*, Lodge's *Rosalynde*, Greene's *Carde of Fancie*, Sidney's *Arcadia*, Spenser's *Faerie Queene* all move slowly. The pace of proceeding is leisurely. In all of them, the time and the space given to physical events is slight compared to the time and space given to what the characters say or think, especially when they say or think in solitude. Clearly it was expected that readers of these romances would be primarily interested in the yearning moods of lonely unfortunates. Place so or so in such or such a situation and see how he calls on his resources of stoicism, or of Christian patience, seems to have been the formula, and the formula could appeal to a tradition antedating Chaucer. But whenever the long speeches of the characters occur there is a shift and lengthening of focus. If in Shakespeare's plays the narrative deposits are Insets, placed at a remove from the dramatic foreground immediacy, then in his—and other authors'—narratives the dramatic deposits are also, in their way, Insets: they recede from the surface of the story.

We said at the outset of this chapter that the narrative and dramatic modes are opposed. So indeed they are, though a narrative frame can contain the dramatic and *vice versa*. When Shakespeare began to write, the narrative mode was ancient; the dramatic (for the Mystery plays were mainly genuine pageants—illustrated stories) very recent. Marlowe's *Tamburlaine* was essentially narrative, and Peele was experimenting adventurously in *The Old Wives' Tale* when the 'Old Wife' breaks off her 'tale' to say 'here they come' as the characters of her narrative enter on the stage to speak in their own persons. The nearest that Shakespeare came to imitating Peele in that method was in *Pericles* which may, in some form, have been conceived and written long before 1609. Meanwhile, between the narrative poems and 1609, Shakespeare mingled the one mode with the other to produce a variety of types of Inset.

III.Kyɔ and the Inset

I

SHAKESPEARE during his career increasingly exploited the Inset as a resource of his dramaturgy and poetics. Not of course only Shakespeare. If the device was opposed to Jonson's craft (Jonson presents a flat surface of word and picture with no hinterland), or too sophisticated for Dekker, and too subtle for Citizen Comedy, it was well-suited to Webster's research into human motives and obscure memory (hence his frequent employment of a traverse), and it offered great temptations to Beaumont and Fletcher at Blackfriars. But then Beaumont and Fletcher had learnt of Shakespeare as Shakespeare had learnt of Beaumont and Fletcher.

But the originator of the Inset had been that "extraordinary dramatic (if not poetic) genius*", Thomas Kyd. He it was who literally *dis*-covered the inner-stage of The Rose theatre† in his conscious determination to activate every level and each playing area of that theatre in *The Spanish Tragedy*. In *The Spanish Tragedy* (as probably in his lost "Hamlet"), and only in a slightly less degree in *Soliman and Perseda*, he visualized main platform, trap-door and cellarage, inner-stage, tarras, the heavens and its supports, in the process of composition and, visualizing them, calculated their scenic and theatrical effectiveness in relation to his book of words. A searching text—a text like a searchlight, seeking out and concentrating first on this level or area of the theatre and then on that, followed by its involvement in the action—sporting Kyd

* T. S. Eliot.
† That The Rose was built by 1588 was proved by E. K. Chambers. See *The Elizabethan Stage*, Vol. II, p. 407.

provided for the Admiral's Men at The Rose. Before *The Spanish Tragedy*, the University Wits had written (except Lyly whose exquisite and adventurous patterns were however designed for performance by boys in an indoor house with, it must be inferred, elaborate *mise-en-scènes*) tragedies consisting of speeches (mostly long, varied occasionally by passages of stychomythia) to be delivered by near stationary actors from a down-centre position on a platform. Certainly such plays were not only Senecan in style of rhetoric, moral sentence and (presumably) gesture but had Senecan physical incidents, violent and bloody. But, as in Seneca, these incidents were a culmination, advance notice of them was given before they arrived, so that when they did arrive they were illustrations to a pre-disclosed argument. Such tragedies were of the kind one might have expected to have been composed for production on a platform in a Cambridge college hall before an academic audience. It was Kyd, who was not a university man, even more than the "upstart Crowe . . . with his Tygers hart wrapt in a Players hide" who showed the Cambridge Wits (and the upstart Crowe) how to use a theatre.

Tamburlaine, both parts, savage and magnificent, had been a platform play. As a play, it does not of course consist solely of language, and the line of story is accompanied by a line of pictures. This latter line was milestoned by some grand spectacles, such as the spectacle of Bajazet and his wife being drawn across the stage by four bitted and bridled captive kings in a wheeled cage. Here the visual display is expansive and lasts longer than the sound track; but this was but large-scale illustration and Marlowe's illustrations, whether expanded or synchronized with the language, were still frontal—platform illustrations illustrating platform poetry. It may be that Marlowe had written the First, and even some of the Second, Part while still at Cambridge, knowing little of the internal structure of The Theatre or The Rose, conceiving the London stage to be simply a wide but shallow platform at one end of a building like the dais of a College hall. Perhaps in fact the stage of The Theatre, when it was first built in 1576, had been no more than such a platform, with entries from side doors and a rear door to a tiring house, but we are obliged to infer—from the stage directions of some of the earliest plays performed there—that the arrangements at The Rose, from the beginning, had been far more elaborate. However that may be, and whether or not Marlowe was limited by a scant knowledge of the London theatres, or by misconception of the different theatres' resources or by inexperience as a dramatist, or by a concentration on his language and the imaginative pictures it discharged rather than on the pictorial setting for the delivery of that language, 1 and 2 *Tamburlaine* are frontal demonstrations. The language is eagerly geographical (no poet approaches Marlowe in his enthusiasm for a real geography) and an intense aspiration expresses itself in vertical images. But Tamburlaine's conquests, actual or desiderated, reveal themselves, on the stage, as a drive to a foreground lateral expansion and the soarings rise from Tamburlaine's, or Marlowe's, temperament and do not rise against a background with imagined degrees of recession. The psychological distance between audience and stage-spectacle is a constant. This constant is conditioned by the plot—one conquest simply precipitating a desire for another, the next—and by the dominant verb appropriate to the plot. The dominant verb of Tamburlaine is 'I will', the intensive form of the Future Indicative: for the hero all along *wills* himself to the point of his career next in advance to that at which he is arrived. The dominance of the Future Indicative in Tamburlaine's speeches encourages, even obliges, a monotony in the vocal style of their delivery.

The verse is delivered within a narrow range of vocal tone and pitch. Now this monoplaned language of *Tamburlaine* corresponds to, is actually adjusted to, its pictorial shallowness —shallowness in the sense of there being only effective forestage *ensemble* and movement. No doubt that in a performance of *Tamburlaine* in the Elizabethan theatre, as in a modern rivival, there would be movements from down-stage to up-stage (and *vice versa*), but such movements would be purely practical rather than visual fulfilments or equivalents of the language. The effective, and illustrative, movement is on or near the apron, is from left to right or right to left, is processional except when it is punctuated by Tamburlaine's declamations to a frozen stage-audience. However, since the word and picture of *Tamburlaine* evince such a correlation there can be no real complaint against Marlowe. In his defence it can be argued that he did not attempt in *Tamburlaine*, except possibly towards the end of Part 2, to explore theatrical (*i.e.* spatial) or linguistic (*i.e.* temporal) gradations of approach or distance.

It is otherwise with Marlowe's later plays. *The Jew of Malta* and *Doctor Faustus* exploit the trap-door, the tarras and the inner-stage to an extent that suggests that Marlowe sought for situations, in the devising of these plays, where he could use these levels and areas. Between *Tamburlaine* and *The Jew of Malta* he had become theatre-minded. But his realization of these structural levels and areas of a theatre—probably of The Rose—extended to an appreciation of actors moving in space. The exploitation of this space was a charge resting on his verse, its responsibility. We put it that movements in depth on the stage, when compelled by the language spoken by the characters, or by their situation, correspond to fluctuations of perspective in the verse, such fluctuations being chiefly occasioned by changes of tense. In brief, Marlowe awoke to the physical properties of the Elizabethan theatre which drove him to try for something other than an animated epic narrative broken into dialogue. In all this it is difficult not to believe that he was inspired by *The Spanish Tragedy*. Kyd, by his example, had shown him how—*how* to use all the resources of the building which was to be the frame and organ of dramatic verse. Directly, or through Marlowe, Kyd also showed *how* to others— Peele, Greene and "the upstart crow", Shakespeare. Kyd's influence was tactical. Given that these other playwrights knew what they wanted to do, what materials they wished to translate from their narrative sources into dramatic terms, Kyd discovered for them methods other than the simple method of following events according to their temporal series.

Kyd had a flair for using every playing-level and playing area of the theatre (main stage, inner-stage, upper galleries and trap-door) and all these are exploited in *The Spanish Tragedy*. He thought up startling situations and saw to it that something was visually happening all the time, that the stage-picture was continually changing. He ensures this either by introducing new persons into the picture or by compelling those persons already on the stage to take up new positions in relation to each other, or—when the picture might have been otherwise rather static—by the sudden adducing of properties, which are either characters' instruments, enlarging their potency, or silent characters in their own right, *e.g.* a book, a dagger, a rope, a letter, a bitten-off tongue. He conceived of the bodies of his characters as mobile objects. More especially, for our purpose, he realized the possibilities of experimenting on the scale of depth—degrees of approach to, or retreat from, the audience—and, scarcely less, the possibilities of vertical differentiation, of contrasting figures on the tarras (or gallery) with figures on the main platform-stage. The English Seneca did not derive his expertise in the manoeuvre of human forms in three-dimensional space from his Roman model whatever else he derived from him—which was considerable. But Kyd's adventures in the physical dimensions of height and depth could not but suggest experiments in the order of time.

If Kyd really supposed (as is likely since others did) that Seneca's Latin imitations of Greek tragedies were actually mounted on a stage, then the supposition must have posed questions: how did Seneca show Hercules demented tearing children to pieces, limb from limb, in full view of an audience? How did Seneca present on the stage a banquet in which a pie is served up compounded of the cooked morsels of a rival's infants?

Assuming that these things were shown, then how? And how to co-ordinate these horrible but fascinating pictures with the massively long speeches which the tragic hero delivers, but with bare opportunities of shifting stance, from a central position on a platform? Sackville and Norton's *Gorboduc* had been near static. The tactical genius of Kyd was directed towards making the violent narrative events of Seneca's radio drama transferable to television—this, and to making a Revenge action, which would play for seventy minutes in a Roman theatre, run to two hours and a half at The Rose in London. The hesitation of an injured hero in Christian times in the light of the Christian injunction against personal revenge solved only one problem. Should he narrate the hanging of Horatio in the bower or show it? By choosing to show it (with the help of a concealed bench on which an actor could stand) he created a purely visual Inset which was never forgotten. Elsewhere, where a previous playwright might have shown Pluto in Hades passing sentence on the newly dead, he chose to narrate.

At the start Kyd 'frames' his play. By arranging that the Ghost of Andrea and Revenge should clamber up from hell (below the trap-door) on to the main stage, where they sit down, one by each of the pillars supporting the heavens,

> to see the misterie,
> And serve for *Chorus* in this Tragedie

he projects his tragedy; the theatre-audience are initially compelled—and the compulsion is maintained throughout, even while the Ghost and Revenge are silent—to "see the misterie" *via* a dead man and a spirit*. This ocular adjustment demanded of the theatre-audience at the outset has its psychological consequence: they are forced into the peculiarly interesting but embarrassing situation of being Peeping Toms and eavesdroppers. Peculiarly interesting, because they are going to see what they do not normally see (things privileged or private); embarrassing, because of the shame—and perhaps guilt—they feel at finding themselves *voyeurs* however unwittingly. Or let us change the 'them' to 'us': *we*, if we translate what we read into performance, are forced into the position of seeing (and hearing) a "misterie" at an apparent remove (at two removes during the play-within-the-play)—which remove turns out not to be a remove but a violation of intimacy. This relationship Kyd establishes at the start by his 'framing'. And the ocular adjustment he exacts, and the psychological adjustments accompanying the ocular adjustment, involve an adjustment in the sense of time.

II

The overall narrative can contain the dramatic; the overall drama can contain the narrative. 'Overall' because it is doubtful whether the two modes—of narrative (third person, past tense, there-then) and drama (first person, present tense, here-now)

---

* Of *The Spanish Tragedy's* induction, Miss M. C. Bradbrook wrote "In this case, the play proper became a play-within-the play on a gigantic scale. Here, as in other inductions, where there was more than a single 'presenter', by remaining on the stage, these characters [here the Ghost and Revenge] commented on the action, and so the two planes of action were felt simultaneously". (See *Themes and Conventions of Elizabethan Tragedy*, pp. 44–45.)

can be mixed or blended in equal proportions, as one can mix or blend currants and raisins—without the issue resulting in a 'no'-form, a medley, a miscellany. The relation, whether in Shakespeare or in other authors, is the relation between a container and a contained: either the thing is an overall narrative containing dramatic Insets or the thing is an overall drama containing narrative Insets. Which of these is Hardy's *The Dynasts* is a problem.

The Inset when it occurs, whether as a dramatic Inset in narrative or a narrative Inset in drama, involves a change of focus. The Inset may be either obtrusive or recessive. In either case it produces a disturbance in the dominant surface of the containing work, and the spectator or listener is compelled to adjust his seeing or hearing (or both): thus the person who reads aloud from a narrative has to adjust his voice when he reaches a passage of dialogue so as to imitate to some extent the voice of the character; thus the actor in a drama, embarking on a passage of narrative, must deviate from the character he has assumed in order to speak in a subtly distinctive voice.

We are not concerned here to trace the history of the dramatic Inset within the narrative, beginning with the *Iliad*, nor with the history of the narrative Inset within the drama beginning with the Messenger's speech in the *Agamemnon*, but simply to observe the mechanics and function of the Inset in Shakespeare. We have seen that in *Venus and Adonis* and *Lucrece* the persons speak much, but that they do so either professedly, or in effect, in isolation from each other, and that their speeches (even when formally duologues) are therefore really monologues— and that monologues, particularly when they belong to the kind known as the Lament (a kind for which Dido's in *Aeneid IV*, after her desertion by Aeneas, presumably provided the pattern for the Middle Ages and Renaissance) are recessive. In contrast, the dramatic Insets in Chaucer's *Miller's Tale* are obtrusive—the speakers Absalon and Alisoun seeming to advance to the foreground when they come to speak in their own persons. "Seeming to advance": they don't really advance. In the theatre, actors may really advance so that the distance between themselves and the audience (but the 'hearers' are spectators!) is reduced. Absalon and Alisoun, and figures in other narratives—verse or prose, e.g. Mrs Croft—come nearer to the audience (genuinely hearers and *not* spectators) when they suddenly speak in their own persons. Yes, but the 'advance', the reduction which changes the 'there-then' to the 'here-now' is a psychological fact which compels a metaphor from optics, and from optics only.

Seeming to 'advance', seeming to 'recede'. We are obliged to employ metaphors—focus, perspective, 'Inset' itself—to describe the effects of the actual grammatical and vocal changes which signalize a switch from narrative to dramatic, from dramatic to narrative.

Yet, when we come to the Insets in Shakespeare's plays, we realize that our terms are not purely metaphorical. Since an audience in a theatre are also really spectators, employing both eye and ear, we find that a Shakespearean Inset is marked off from its context, not only by an actor's change of voice and attitude, but (often) by a physical grouping or re-distribution on the stage, so as to provide an impression of an altered focus, of a variation in the play's customary or dominant distance from the spectator. A picture within a picture results.

Admittedly narrative passages, marked off from, and yet related to, their surround are not the only kind of pictorial Inset in the plays. That theatrical performance, 'The Murder of Gonzago' in *Hamlet*, was presumably enacted on the inner stage of the Elizabethan theatre, and that inner stage—a framed recession—set at one remove from the stage audience composed of Claudius and his court, and at two removes from the paying audience in the theatre, provides a good analogy with the inset of our imagined Florentine painting of the Visitation*. But not only is it a genuine pictorial Inset, for in other ways—stylistic and vocal—'The Murder of Gonzago' is marked off from its surround, and the fact that this device of a play-within-the-play may have been *derived*, or copied, from

---

* 'Presumably' enacted on the inner stage. Should the celebrant of the holy sacrifice of the mass stand with his back to the congregation or facing them? It is possible that 'The Murder of Gonzago' was played centre and down—far down—stage (near the modern footlights) and that the stage audience sat above on the tarras, or lords' room, the balcony and adjoining galleries, looking down and facing the paying audience. But how then would Hamlet's cuddly and naughty badinage with Ophelia be vocally projected? Shouted? Not likely. The problem is further discussed. pp. 131–135.

Kyd's 'Hamlet' or from his *Spanish Tragedy* is irrelevant. It is the particular Shakespearean result we are considering, and in the result 'The Murder of Gonzago' is—no less than narrative Insets—set off from its surround. As with a narrative Inset the stage audience, in 'The Murder of Gonzago', are transformed to a mute and frozen group—that is, until Claudius can bear the spectacle and the language no longer and, starting up, shatters the Inset with his cry of "Give me some Light. Away". Further, and again as in a narrative Inset, the speech is here distinguished from the containing and—occasionally—inter-jecting dialogue. The players, playing professional Players, declaim in a consciously heightened and histrionic manner (not, despite Hamlet's advice, "trippingly on the tongue") while Claudius is made to peer into his past or, rather, is nudged nastily to a point where, it appears to him, it cannot be coincidence—someone else knows, and this activates his memory. For, as in a narrative Inset, a time—other than the stage *now*—is invoked, a stretch of history, "writ in choice Italian", dangerously like an episode out of Claudius' past, is summoned*.

Besides framed narrative and the framed 'play-within-the-play' Shakespeare can create Insets of other kinds. There are the songs. His songs interrupt the flow of spoken blank verse. With shorter lines, formal rhyme and distinctive vocal 'gear', these genuine lyrics do not however merely interrupt the blank verse but introduce a new plane. Planes are not only a matter of higher and lower, but relate to the other dimension expressed by the comparatives further and nearer. Shakespeare's songs, while being sung, effect a change in the pictorial surface presented to the audience. Whether that change is one of advance or recession is open to discussion in the light of any particular song, for the songs indeed vary. A song may be more or less obviously articulated to the plot line; it might be so well joined as a member of the plot line that its omission might lead the audience into doubt as to the succession of events; or a song

---

* I am here (as elsewhere) reminded of S. L. Bethell's *Shakespeare and the Popular Dramatic Tradition*. "an audience watches a stage audience watching a play, and so becomes simultaneously aware of three planes of reality". I would account Bethell's book, and especially its discussion of Multi-Consciousness, as a fruitful source of some of my own thinking.

KYD AND THE INSET

may seem to be no more than a *divertissement* or a stop gap; but elsewhere its function is neither to forward the plot nor to delay it. The songs in *Twelfth Night* give depth to the play, not in spite of, but because they are apparently irrelevant to all the goings on of the foreground action.

But while other kinds of Inset will be considered*, it is proper to treat of the narrative kind first, if only because Shakespeare, at the outset of a career, was confronted with sources in the form of narratives. "How can I turn this *novella*, or those pages of Hall or Holinshed, into a play—how dramatize this narrative?" was necessarily the prime question before he began each new composition. Certainly this must have become increasingly a *tactical* question, to be answered with increasing assurance—even instinctively—as experience gathered. Nevertheless, the narrative sources must have offered degrees of resistance to translation, or rather transmutation, into the dramatic pronoun and tense, with its extra dimension of sight, and while there were few limits—in that period of theatrical history—as to what could be shown, there would be choices open as to what ought to be shown, what told. On other occasions there were no choices—or there seemed none. Thus: you cannot show a ship-wreck, but you can describe one after it has happened, seems to have been a tactical conclusion before the composition of *Twelfth Night*. But this conclusion was to be reversed, some ten or eleven years later, when it came to *The Tempest*. Next, a narrative could be, and in the case of the Renaissance narrative concerning romantic love (though especially if set in pastoral surroundings where there was much yearning and groaning and moaning by lover for absent beloved) habitually was, conducted at an extremely leisurely pace so that a speeding-up in the process of dramatic translation was essential. Time intervals were reduced. Thus the events of Brooke's poem *Romeus and Juliet* take place over a period of nine months; in Shakespeare's *Romeo and Juliet* they take place in two or three days and nights, especially in the nights. The economy of the Renaissance historian was of course different. His narrative was more controlled by the pulse of history:

---

* But not the sermon (*e.g.* Jacques on the Seven Ages in *As You Like It*), nor the lecture (*e.g.* Ulysses on Time), for neither of these have a genuine narrative line.

events in a decade of English history had been either crowded or slack.

Whatever the choices open, the narrative was generally more comprehensive than the resulting play. It could afford to be as the play could not. Hence the problem, as far as the earlier plays go, would probably have been this: "Your narrative source covers XYZ but I can only show Y and part of Z. X then, in so far as it is necessary for the understanding of Y, must be narrated." Hence the expository speeches in the first scenes of Shakespeare's early plays. Now these expository speeches form one type of narrative Inset. But, from the practice of this type, exercise in it, there appeared the possibility of other types. Even the original expository type, though it persists to the end, underwent considerable development.

IV. The Expository Inset

I. A LONG STORY

IN THE *Comedy of Errors*, Act I, sc. i, Egeon, a Syracusan, is sentenced to death by the Duke of Ephesus. The rulers of Syracuse have been cruel to citizens from Ephesus and so this sentence on a citizen from Syracuse is a reprisal. Yet the Duke gives the doomed Egeon an opportunity to explain why he risked his life by coming to Ephesus:

> Well, Siracusian, say in briefe the cause
> Why thou departedst from thy native home?
> And for what cause thou cam'st to Ephesus.

It must be confessed that, although Egeon's reply takes up 103 of the total of 147 lines of the scene, he is "brief" in that an exceedingly complicated background story is narrated without a line to spare. He is long in that his narration is utterly flat and colourless. It is so because of the absence of variation of pace and tone, because of the absence of vivid realization of detail through the power of description (that power which Shakespeare—more than any—was to exercise with such abundant, such sovereign, ease) and because of the near absence of variation of tense and grammatical construction—and these three absences are inter-related. The presence of one would have involved the presence of the other two. Co-relative with the linguistic—the sonic—dullness is the theatrical—the visual—dullness: unless the stage producer can contrive—deliberately—to manage variations of position, Egeon must remain rooted beside his gaoler at one spot. His stage auditors must also stand rooted. Egeon's story was a challenge to Shakespeare's skill because of the need to leave his audience at the end in no doubt as to who was who and who is who. The

41

story is puzzling, like that kind of riddle which begins "Brothers and sisters have I none/But that man's father is my father's son", and, despite the sonic and visual dullness, Shakespeare has been astoundingly skilful in making it clear that the speaker, Egeon, had had twin-sons, that these twin-sons had been attended by a pair of twin-brothers, that—because of a shipwreck nearly twenty-three years ago—the speaker and one of his sons, accompanied by one of the servants, had been separated from his wife, his other son and the remaining servant; that, on becoming eighteen years old, his son—the one who had stayed with Egeon—attended by his servant, had set off each to find his lost brother and had never returned; and that he—the speaker—had in turn, for the last five years, been roving the world in search of this son and his servant and had at last come to Ephesus and there been arrested as a Syracusan. Shakespeare's expository skill is here as striking as is his poetic and dramatic dullness.

The skill in making all this clear *at a single hearing* is the more impressive when one realizes—although the place-names Syracuse, Epidamnus and Corinth are mentioned—that this family history is conveyed without bringing in a single personal name. Since both the narrator's sons were called Antipholus and both their servants Dromio that may have been wise. The writer of narrative in verse can be more economic than the writer of prose narrative. Shakespeare here has been as economic as possible. This could be tested: Ask anyone to give Egeon's story in his own words and, struggling to avoid the listener's, and his own, confusion, he will take a long time— much longer than Shakespeare—in the telling. Compare Shakespeare's expository skill with that of Gower, who provided Shakespeare's source. Gower is a finer poet than is usually allowed, but he rambles and Shakespeare did more than modernize. He did more by doing less.

While admiring Shakespeare's extraordinary skill in telling a long and complicated story very simply and directly (giving the lie to Matthew Arnold's complaints that "he seemed to have tried all styles except the style of simplicity" and "he seemed incapable of saying anything in a straightforward manner") in this initial scene of the play where an exposition of a past—Egeon's past—is essential for the understanding of

what we are about to hear and see, it must still be admitted
that the speech is of deadly flatness and colourlessness. Now is
this exactly the penalty Shakespeare has to pay for such a
sheerly economic presentation of material?

Flat and, because flat, colourless? 'Flat' and 'colourless' are
both, of course, metaphors. We are obliged, along with everyone else, to resort to metaphors when an attempt is made to
describe that unique thing—the style of a literary passage.
But Egeon's narrative is not just a literary passage. It is—or
was—vocal, something sounded aloud and, as such, was
strictly monotonous for 'stylistic' reasons now to be discussed.
It was also flat and motionless. Linguistic, and so vocal,
monotony: though Egeon draws on the deep backward and
abysm of time, as Prospero is to do later, he does not once hale
the 'then' and 'there' into the 'here' and 'now' through
employing the historic present (whereby that which is past and
dead is, in a manner, re-lived) as does Prospero*. Instead the
past is firmly and finally relegated to the past:

> My youngest boy, and yet my eldest care,
> At eighteen yeeres became inquisitive
> After his brother; and importun'd me
> That his attendant, so his case was like,
> Reft of his brother, but retain'd his name,
> Might beare him company in the quest of him:
> Whom whil'st I laboured of a love to see,
> I hazarded the losse of whom I lov'd . . .
>
> I. i. 125–132

Are then the 103 lines—broken only twice, and then very
briefly, by the Duke of Ephesus simply to urge Egeon to keep
on talking—really a part of the dramatic reality of *Comedy of
Errors* at all? Or is their function merely that of a Prologue, an
Induction, comparable to the function of the sonnet prefacing
Romeo and Juliet or of the Chorus before Act I of *Henry V*?

Not exactly: for Egeon, who makes his first appearance in the
first scene of the play, makes his second appearance in the last.
Not able to muster his ransom, he is brought out to execution,
his whole intervening time having been spent in prison. Then,

---

* The nearest that is reached is the use of three or four present participles,
e.g. 'fainting', 'sinking-ripe', 'gazing'. But in Egeon's story these are
clearly adjectives—adjectives within sentences that are framed in the past.

all the "errors" of the Comedy of Errors rectified, he is presumably reprieved, though we are not told so. Indeed, having established identities, following the confusion arising out of the deployment of two sets of twins, he is strangely disregarded and lapses into silence. Still, in the final scene of the *Comedy*, he is a character of sorts, and this prevents us from asserting that his 103 lines in Act I, sc. i, constitute a Prologue and nothing else. He is a figure in the picture and not a Guide at the Louvre explaining to his audience what to look for. Even so, until he is led on in the final scene, simply to identify and to be identified, he is effectually suspended from the dramatic reality of the comedy. Having given the audience the background to the situation, he is dismissed from mind and the audience settles down to enjoy Shakespeare's version of Plautus' *Menaechini*.

So, if these lines, though they deliver a factual background with amazing efficiency, remain outside the dramatic reality, serving rather as a kind of prologue, and are in themselves both colourless and flat, they scarcely create an Inset. Nevertheless Egeon's narrative—referring, as it does, to times and places remote from the dramatic here and now of its delivery—is mechanically an Inset. It is adduced here as the example of the type of the Expository Inset. Shakespeare was going to feel the necessity of an Expository Inset at the start of nearly every play succeeding *The Comedy of Errors* which he undertook. Increasingly he was to 'set' the expository narrative at a different plane of distance from the spectator than the purely dramatic which followed and which yet, in terms of overall, was to contain it. Egeon's narrative is, then, an Inset (or it introduces one), if only for mechanical reasons, but, because of its linguistic (and so vocal, and so theatrical) substance, it is a frame too detached and too shallow in relation to the picture it contains.

In his possibly first play, Shakespeare was encountering difficulties because he was ambitious, because he was not content with giving a simple English version of Plautus' *Menaechmi*, but aimed at a refinement or development which involved blending the substance of the plot of the Roman play with a narrative supplied by Gower. In the result the Gower component remains a narrative. Yet, if the Inset of *Comedy of*

Errors I. i. is shallow and detached, it gave him experience in a method, a non-dramatic method, and in subsequent plays, when confronted with the same need to give information to his audience at the outset, he developed the Expository Inset so that—besides imparting information necessary for the understanding of the plot—it lived on to create a hinterland to what followed, commenting on the foreground action.

And here it should be recalled that Shakespeare, or some other dramatist associated with Shakespeare, returned to Gower's narrative of Apollonius of Tyre for the composition of *Pericles*. Gower then appears downstage in person and the scenes are set in remote perspective from the audience. In *Pericles*, as nowhere else in Shakespeare, the stage pictures and the stage dialogue are presented, as it were, as a series of illustrations or Insets to Gower's story. In *Pericles*, it is Gower who is in the foreground while the persons of his story are set remotely in the past and in the background*.

II. ROYAL PROGRESS

Shakespeare was not always to present his Expository Inset in Act I, sc.i. In I. ii. of *The Tempest*, Prospero delivers a narrative, drawn from "the dark-backward and Abisme of Time", the substance of which is nearly as complicated as Egeon's. It follows a short opening scene crammed with violent movement, a scene which is itself to be referred to in the narrative as the culmination of a long train of previous events leading to the moment of the narration. If Prospero's tale seems more complicated and more physically eventful than Egeon's (though it is not), this is because Prospero's Inset possesses a variety of forms of the past tense, each with its appropriate vocal tone, that Egeon's does not have†.

But that an Expository Inset can be delayed until after Act I requires, it would seem, this condition: the Inset must then narrate a single main event that took place previous to events

---

* For a fuller discussion see pp.148–156 below.

† For an account of the difference of grammatical forms in the two Insets see *Poets' Grammar: Person, Time and Mood in Poetry* (Routledge & Kegan Paul) 1958, pp. 75–78 and, for the consequent difference of vocal utterance, *Poetry and the Physical Voice* (Routledge & Kegan Paul) 1962, p. 158.

shown on the stage. This alone justifies an elaborate telling *in medias res* shown. Perhaps the only instance is Enobarbus' account of the lovers' first meeting in *Antony and Cleopatra*, II. ii.

The classification of this Inset as Expository might be disputed. For while Enobarbus' description of Antony and Cleopatra's first meeting is not plot-required (as the Queen's account of Ophelia's drowning is plot-required), since that first meeting took place anterior to events shown on the stage, neither is its main function (it could be argued) expository since the audience—or both audiences—have already been able to understand what is going on in *Antony and Cleopatra* for two acts, without the information it supplies, and could manage without it for three acts more. But there are yet stronger objections to considering Enobarbus' 'first meeting' as a Voluntary*. It does not introduce into *Antony and Cleopatra*—as the 'Queen Mab' Voluntary introduces into *Romeo and Juliet* or as the 'fictive sister' Voluntary introduces into *Twelfth Night*—a mythical or human figure supernumerary to the *dramatis personae* and apparently foreign to his or her setting.

What the account of Enobarbus does is to satisfy curiosity to the full. 'How did it start? Where did it all begin?' are the questions asked by nearly all women (if not men) of any amorous affair, scandalous or romantic, they hear about, especially if one—or even both—of the lovers is royal. This inquisitiveness about the *origin* of an 'affair' may seem sentimental, prying or undignified if we read the daily papers or the women's weeklies. The inquisitiveness has at least this justification—no beginning, no affair. But is an affair or romance, even a royal one, important enough to deserve this curiosity? The affair between Antony and Cleopatra was important historically: it is regarded as politically significant in the terms of the play and—outside the play—it provoked results which still perhaps reverberate. If in II. ii. Enobarbus satisfies the curiosity of the theatre audience as to how and where it all began, he also satisfies the curiosity of his stage-audience which consists not of women but of the Romans, Agrippa and Mecenas. Moreover, Agrippa and Mecenas were both

---

* See p.12 for a description of the Voluntary and pp.76 ff. for a study of examples.

inquisitive enough to have listened to gossip about the first meeting earlier:

Mecenas: She's a most triumphant Lady, if report be square to her.
Enobarbus: When she first met Marke Anthony, she purst up his heart upon the River of Sidnis.
Agrippa: There she appear'd indeed: or my reporter devis'd well for her.

Agrippa is eager to have his "reporter" confirmed from an 'inside source'. Inasmuch as that 'first meeting' was the original occasion for all that is shown in the course of five acts—which it is—the Inset can fairly be regarded as mainly expository in function; nor, since that occasion was single and simple (*a* first meeting being assumed if not realized by a theatre-audience whose normal curiosity would nevertheless become aroused at some point after they had once become interested in the lovers), was it necessary to advance it to Act I. The retardation brings its advantages.

Interest in the *origin* of an amorous affair or romance is not however limited to those who report it and to those who listen, gossip and speculate about it. The origin of 'their' affair is usually of intense interest to the lovers themselves and they like to hold on to memories of their 'first meeting' quite grimly until death do them part. Their final memories may be of their first meeting. This indeed is the case with Cleopatra, for in V. ii., immediately after resolving on suicide, she commands Charmian

> Go fetch
> My best Attyres. I am againe for Cidnus,
> To meete Marke Anthony.*

and she would feel "base" if Charmian should die before herself and so "*first meete* the Curled Anthony".

There is then an advantage in delaying Enobarbus' Inset. Purely as an Exposition it can be withheld until after Act I, and this withholding narrows the gap of effectiveness—i.e. just as a rhyme cannot be detected if its pair of elements are separated by too many intervening lines so neither can other kinds of linguistic and dramatic concordance—between

---

* Both in II. ii. and V. ii. 'Cydnus' appears as 'Cidrus' in the First Folio. The compositor was not knowledgeable in foreign place-names.

Enobarbus' Inset of the 'first meeting' upon the 'River of Cydnus' and the after death 'first meeting' in V. ii.* Cleopatra togs up in her "best Attyres" since she is "againe for Cydnus"; and her "dream" of an Antony, whose "legges bestrid the Ocean" and whose "rear'd arme/Crested the world", has so much the more beautiful power because the theatre-audience connects *this* 'first meeting' with the original 'first meeting' as narrated by Enobarbus. Even if the main function of Enobarbus' Inset is Expository (presenting the theatre-audience with information about a situation that started before Act I. i.), Shakespeare, at this stage of his career, is not going to limit the device so that it produces only a local effect. This Expository has 'side effects', 'side effects' which may indeed gather in importance beyond the principal intention. Among its 'side effects' this Expository contains properties which one might have considered the special prerogatives of either the Plot-required or the Voluntary Insets: of the Plot-required, because that 'first meeting', which could have ante-dated I. i. by any number of days or years, is remembered by Cleopatra in V. ii. so as to become the motive behind her togging up; of the Voluntary, because it "bodies forth" a 'picture' with a life of its own (so that it could exist on its own as a complete 'pictorial' poem) and because it could be 'cut' in a performance of the play, despite its connection with V. ii., without any injury to the audience's pursuit of the plot-line.

Egypt and Rome: "look here upon this picture and on this". *Antony and Cleopatra* of course exhibits the confrontation between Western Rome, energetic and dutiful, and the East where the beds are soft. But though Rome and Egypt are, within the design of the play, opposed, the nature of the opposition is such that when the scene is laid in Egypt then Rome—physically remote—is in a sense, always *there*, obtruding itself.

It is of course natural when a pair of lovers are separated that one should think about and imagine the other in his or her

---

* In Shakespeare's source, North's translation of Plutarch's *Lives*, the first meeting is given in its chronological place (i.e. there is no 'flash-back'). Shakespeare's "verbal borrowing" (see *Shakespeare's Plutarch* ed. by C. F. Tucker Brooke (Chatto & Windus) 1909, p. xi) from North may be intense here but (i) his transposition of the episode, and (ii) his retention of its narrative presentation, were decisive acts of genius.

setting: and it is not merely natural but it is convenient for Shakespeare, or any dramatist, one would suppose, that it should be natural. In the design of many of Shakespeare's plays there is frequently an opposition of places with such an opposition involving the spatial division of lovers—e.g. Verona/ Mantua, Venice/Belmont, Troy/the Grecian Camp, Venice/ Cyprus—but, despite this frequency, a sense of the opposing place occluding or dispossessing the one which is actually being presented on the stage occurs infrequently and, when it does, it is not sustained*. In *Antony and Cleopatra* it is a different matter: Antony, leaving Cleopatra for Rome, says:

> Our separation so abides and flies,
> That thou reciding heere, goes yet with mee;
> And I hence fleeting, heere remaine with thee.
>
> I. iii.

and not only does Cleopatra go with him to Rome, but also her setting, Egypt; and when he is in Egypt his mind is—more often than not—in Rome, so that Cleopatra can fairly complain:

> He was dispos'd to mirth, but on the sodaine
> A Romaine thought hath strooke him.

When the lovers are together in Egypt, Rome—and Roman Fulvia or Roman Octavius Caesar—is from the beginning continually impinging, interrupting, preventing their enjoyment of each other. They scarcely get a moment's peace and privacy!—what with (i) Antony's conscience (and an uneasy conscience always betokens a *divided* man) about Fulvia and duty, with (ii) the interruption of messengers—bearing unpleasant messages—from Rome, and with (iii) the final invasion of Egypt by Octavius Caesar and his army. The lovers never enjoy a moment's peace together and when they are divided in space—Antony in Rome, Cleopatra in Egypt—they are no happier either. In Rome, Antony wishes himself in Egypt; in Egypt, Cleopatra violently upsets herself at the

---

* An example is Bassanio, in Venice, discoursing on "a lady richly left" in Belmont—but Belmont is not imaginatively realized (*Merchant of Venice*, I. i.). Romeo in Mantua has a dream of Juliet, but neither Juliet nor Verona are realized (*Romeo and Juliet*, V. i.).

thought of Antony with his new wife, Octavia. Still, it is not only in Antony's personality, when he is in Rome, that the memory—the desire and the vision—works: Cleopatra-Egypt (or Egypt-Cleopatra) works, if not as a delicious *memory* (for Agrippa and Mecenas had not seen Cleopatra to remember though they remembered the reports of those who had), then as a beguiling lure in the minds of all Romans in Rome itself or beyond its walls. This attraction that Cleopatra-Egypt has for the Romans may express itself in the form of puritan disapproval unless they are drunk (II. ii.) and then the attraction, and so the envy for Antony (who never had a moment's peace with Cleopatra because of his domestic and political conscience), is positively released. On the other side, it is not the case that all the Egyptians are possessed by the glamour of Rome and western technology—for there was no glamour—but Cleopatra, almost at the end, was possessed by the geographical fact of Rome; and that fact, so forcefully realized that its picture blocks the Egyptian scene, was restrictive, destructive and, ultimately, unpleasant. *Here* (in Egypt) she can see herself and Iras *there* (in Rome) as prisoners:

> Now Iras, what think'st thou?
> Thou, an Egyptian Puppet shall be shewne
> In Rome as well as I: Mechanicke Slaves
> With greazie Aprons, Rules, and Hammers shall
> Uplift us to the view. In their thicke breathes,
> Ranke of grosse dyet, shall we be enclowded,
> And forc'd to drinke their vapour.

and she can foresee herself *there* watching herself being enacted on the Roman stage:

> I shall see
> Some squeaking Cleopatra Boy my greatnesse
> I'th' posture of a Whore.

Many, if not most, of Shakespeare's plays are constructed on a two-place or a here/there principle and not only the comedies (consider *Henry V*: England/France, *Macbeth*: Scotland/England), but in no other play does the *contemporary* 'there' so continuously invade the 'here' of the actual scene to trouble or to enchant as in *Antony and Cleopatra*.

Nevertheless, there is a difference in the manner that the 'there' invades according as to whether the 'here' happens to be Egypt or Rome. When the scene is in Egypt, the 'there' of Rome presents itself as a pull on Antony; this pull resisted, Rome advances from a wing to occlude and then destroy; but when the scene is laid in Rome, the 'there' of Egypt is variously a luring dream or vision, the dream or vision—emanating from memory or bred out of desire—projects itself as a kind of vibrating, translucent yet pictorial, curtain between the Roman scene and the theatre-audience. "How did the affair begin?", the theatre- and the stage-audience tacitly ask. "I will tell you", replies Enobarbus (down centre) and, with only an occasional glance at his stage-auditors, Agrippa and Mecenas, to measure their response, he projects his Inset:

> The Barge she sat in, like a burnisht Throne
> Burnt on the water . . .

and the 'there' hovers in front of, and then masks, the 'here'—the Roman scene, the physical background. The Egyptian picture which Enobarbus projects is for him a memory. He was an eye-witness 'there' and *then*. He refers to a time earlier than the time-sequence of the play, but, as he projects the memory, it becomes again *present*, and the verbs move forward in time from their past inflections to present inflections. The perfects "sat", "Burnt", the frequent "were", the ambi-temporal "beate", the emphatic present perfects "did lye", "did seeme", "did coole" give way to the great present tense forms of

> At the Helme
> A seeming Mer-maide *steeres*: The Silken Tackle,
> *Swell* with the touches of those Flower-soft hands,
> That yarely *frame* the office. From the Barge
> A strange invisible perfume *hits* the sense
> Of the adjacent Wharfes.*

as the 'there and then' becomes 'here and now'. Next the verbs return to a mixture of the narrative perfects, the ambi-temporal "did sit", the pluperfect "had gone", the short-cut perfects,

* The italics in quotations are throughout mine. The italicized personal names of the Folio are here given in roman.

the present participles, but concludes again in the present tense:

> our Courteous Anthony
> Whom nere the word of 'No' woman heard speake,
> Being barber'd ten times o're, *goes* to the Feast;
> And for his ordinary, *paies* his heart,
> For what his eyes *eate* onely.

Certainly the picture of this Inset, which casts the physical stage-picture (for both audiences) into an "Oblivion", for the duration of the Inset's existence, has the radiating influence which is a mark of the Voluntary (since this Inset is recalled, in V. ii. with "I am againe for Cydnus") and it contributes to the 'here-there', 'there-here' structure of the play. Nevertheless, it is Expository in that it satisfies curiosity in answering the question 'How did it all begin?'

III. THE ADVENTUROUS CAREER

Some five years before *Antony and Cleopatra*, Shakespeare had ventured an Inset which, though delayed, was Expository in its principal function and yet has some characteristics of the Voluntary. I refer to Othello's story (Act I, sc. iii) of his wooing of Desdemona. Because this story is his form of defence when on trial before the Duke and Senators of Venice on a charge of "witchcraft" ('black' magic) its essentially narrative nature is masked. The story is 'dramatized', partly because its unfolding is broken by questions put to Othello and observations passed on his story by members of his interior audience, and partly because Othello's trial is a component in the "swelling Act", a cause of the emerging here and now of the plot of the drama. Despite this, the story is primarily a narrative of a there and then in the past tense. The story is another Shakespearean 'purple' passage, as they say. Now why is it that so many of the 'purple' (which is not to say 'best' but something like it) passages are Insets? Because they call on the powers of the narrative, as opposed to the dramatic, poet? The question cannot be answered unless to remark that with such Insets Shakespeare had to fight against the plain daylight physical scene the audience saw before them; fight against that to give a 'picture' that supplanted what physically confronted them.

Othello's tale of his "whole course of love" is like Enobarbus' Inset in that it explains to two audiences *viz.* (i) an audience seated in the body of the theatre and (ii) an interior audience, here seated ceremonially on the stage, how 'it all began'. Depending on its reaction to Othello's "round un-varnish'd Tale", this interior (or stage-) audience will adjudge the 'affair' to be either 'scandalous' or 'romantic'. But the *Othello* Inset is unlike Enobarbus' in two respects. For Othello does not describe pictorially the physical surroundings that attended the lovers' 'first meeting', nor does he describe Desdemona's person or dress, though we infer she was meek and given to admiration. Neither deeply interested Othello. Moreover, because Othello's narrative was a defence against a criminal charge, it is altogether more dramatically built in; he is not a mere witness, as was Enobarbus, but personally interested. He is one of the pair of lovers. Nevertheless one supposes that Antony's description of his first sight of Cleopatra in her barge would have corresponded with Enobarbus' since Cleopatra affected Antony as she affected Enobarbus the mere witness.

Othello's tale of "his whole course of love" resembles Enobarbus' account of Antony's first meeting with Cleopatra in that it tells the internal audience consisting of Duke and Senators—arrayed and arranged on the stage—and the containing theatre-audience alike, 'how it all began', but is more directly Expository. In *Antony and Cleopatra* the need to inform the theatre-audience 'how it all began' was not indeed obligatory, and the stage-audience of Romans had already heard reports before. So the Voluntary element is pronounced. In *Othello* the stage-audience is ignorant, and although it can suppose a wooing, the manner of that wooing (was it "black magic"?) needs exposition. That is the plot situation, but it is also the situation of the theatre-audience: no less than the stage-audience the theatre-audience wants its curiosity gratified, but it does not end there. There is the situational point: Othello needs to clear himself of a charge, to show himself as being candid (i.e. 'white') in motive and method in addition to gratifying curiosity. It is this need which forbids the delay of the *Othello* Exposition later than Act I.

And that leads to the points of unlikeness. Not only is the stage-audience in *Othello* ignorant and, though ignorant, hostile or neutral (while the other stage-audience in *Antony and Cleopatra* had been primed to receive, what it had already heard before, with favour), but it listens—not to a tale of the impact of a near-sorceress on a man (and that man a Roman hero) on a single occasion—judicially to a "tale" of how a man was not a sorcerer but impressed a girl by talking about himself not on one occasion but "oft". But the setting of each occasion was the same—Brabantio's house. Moreover the deployment of the figures in that setting was the same on each occasion: we are presented with the picture of a Desdemona, sitting silent and enraptured at the feet of Othello, 'devouring up' his discourse between interruptions caused by "house Affaires". (Did Othello take these interruptions well? Did he continue with his adventures in her absence, with reduced fervour, to Brabantio?) The effect is of multiplicity consolidated into unity. "Oft" he told "the Storie" of his life but the Inset picture is constant. This effect is secured by the clash of tenses. The wooing and winning are past and the containing tense is in the pretorite: "Wherein I *spoke* ...", "It was my hint to speake ...", "She gave me for my paines a world of kisses ...", but the substance of his story is still continuing in the exotic spaces where Othello *had* once travelled: the heads of the hills still "*touch* heaven", the cannibals still "each other eate" and the heads of the Antropophagie still "Doe grow beneath their shoulders". Othello's Exposition is a story within a story, but the stuff of the innermost story instead of being thrust back into a remote pluperfect "had" is even now happening. It is this presence of his past which enchanted Desdemona and now captivates the Duke and Senators. Othello's hardships and achievements, though long past, still smart; they lie near enough to be invoked, and *are* invoked at each crisis—to his advantage, for the gain of a mixed pity and admiration.

As Enobarbus' account is revived again in Act V, sc. ii of *Antony and Cleopatra* so Othello's "story" is not sealed after its telling. In his final speech (V. ii.) he narrates what he did "in Aleppo once" to "a malignant and a Turbond-Turke". This recalls the narrative of his adventures in I. iii. (where he narrates to the Senators what he had narrated to Desdemona). He goes back again to his colourful past. The Levant and the Traducing Muslim, if not so exotic, are more glamorous than the anthropophegie and the cannibals. Othello's love ended as it began—by a dependence, for effect, on a romantic (and heroic) past which was completed before the action of the play starts. Both audiences will realize this.

* * *

The Expository Inset in *Othello*, broken by passages of dialogue, is nearly disguised as dramatic exchange. Yet it is essentially narrative. As with other Insets an imaginative picture is superimposed on an actual. The actual picture is formal and ceremonial—rows of seated figures exercising a judicial function with a standing defendant confined and near motionless. Contrasted with this is a picture of a domestic interior, representative of many occasions, which is not static because of Othello's large gestures and Desdemona's periodic retreats to the kitchen. The stage-audience are persuaded of the truth and honesty of the Inset picture; the theatre-audience, at one remove, regard it with more detachment.

V. The Interior Plot-required Inset

To be distinguished from the expository narration of past events, of a history, of data which the audience must grasp before the play begins, is the narrative which refers, not to events anterior to the matter now to be dramatically presented, but to events which happen within the temporal span of the dramatic action, where the dramatic poet turns narrative poet because either he cannot show them on the stage or he chooses not to show them. Ophelia's suicide by drowning could not be shown on the stage, though it happened during the action, and therefore it was narrated; Hamlet's fight with the sea-pirates, on his way to England, could perhaps have been shown but Shakespeare preferred the indirect means of narrating it. This kind is the Interior Plot-required Inset.

1. THE MOCKED KING

An early instance of this kind occurs in *3 Henry VI* when the baiting of York is narrated (II. i.). What is strange is that this narrative Inset is preceded (I. iv.) by a scene which dramatically presents this killing. Why this reinforcement? What is the relation between (*a*) the killing of York shown, and (*b*) the killing of York told? Such questions arise as well as the more general question of the relation between an Interior Plot-required Inset and the play in which it occurs, and the question of the distinction in nature as well as function between the Expository and the Internal Plot-required Insets.

In considering these questions, with reference to our example, I shall leave aside the vexed, or formerly vexed, dispute as to authorship. Without calling the evidence, I shall assume

3 Henry VI to be Shakespeare's because he either wrote it or because, in re-writing the work of other men, he made it his own.

In *3 Henry VI*, I. iv. the baiting and killing of York is first *dramatized*—the "action is suited to the word, the word to the action", the 'here' and the 'now' are shown, the linguistic and the pictorial are synchronized. Because the moment is shown in the inflexions of the language and their mode of utterance have the special urgency of a containing present (*past* grievances or causes of vengeance are of course invoked, but they re-*present* themselves in the moment by moment dramatic fury) or imperative grammatical tense.

Thus the dementedly vindictive Queen Margaret cries:

> Brave Warriors, Clifford and Northumberland,
> Come make him stand upon this Mole-hil here,
>
> (66–67)

and it is clear that Clifford and Northumberland promptly execute her command, for by her fifth line:

> What, was it you that would be Englands King?

York *has* been set upon the 'molehill' (in the implicit stage-direction the representation of some kind of hillock or mound is required). Margaret next taunts him:

> Where are your Messe of Sonnes, to back you now?
> The wanton Edward, and the lustie George?
> And where's that valiant Crook-back Prodigie,
> Dickie, your Boy, that with his grumbling voyce
> Was wont to cheare his Dad in Mutinies?
>
> (73–77)

Then she offers him a handkerchief stained with the blood of his twelve-years' old son:

> . . . where is your Darling, Rutland?
> Looke Yorke, I stayn'd this Napkin with the blood
> That valiant Clifford, with his Rapiers point,
>   Made issue from the Bosome of the Boy:
> And if thine eyes can water for his death,
> I give thee this to drie thy Cheekes withall.
>
> (78–83)

but since York does not 'rise' to the 'she-wolf's' torment, either by word or tear, at the sight of the 'napkin', and refuses to accept it, she is nettled the more:

> What, hath thy fierie heart so parcht thine entrayles,
> That not a Teare can fall, for Rutlands death?
> Why art thou patient, man? thou should'st be mad:
> And I, to make thee mad, doe mock thee thus.
> Stampe, rave, and fret, that I may sing and dance.
> Thou would'st be fee'd, I see, to make me sport:
> Yorke cannot speake, unlesse he weare a Crowne.
> A Crowne for Yorke; and Lords, bow lowe to him:
> Hold you his hands, whilst I doe set it on.
>
> (87-95)

Here, according to most modern editions, Margaret puts "a paper crown on his head"*, and she and the others do a mock obeisance to him. York at last is driven beyond silent endurance —gratifying his tormentors thereby in so weakening—so that he upbraids, rips off the crown from his brows, and curses the "ruthless Queen" and the "hard-hearted Clifford". The expression of his woes impels one of his torturers, Northumberland, to compassion (the Queen jeers: "What, weeping-ripe, my Lord *Northumberland*?"), but it inflames the other two yet more. Clifford and the Queen stab the sufferer and the scene concludes with Margaret's grim joke:

> Off with his Head, and set it on Yorke Gates,
> So Yorke may over-looke the Towne of Yorke.

This was—or is—the dramatic showing of the event.

Before looking at the narrative Inset of this event in the following (II. i.) scene, it is worth reminding ourselves that Shakespeare—for this incident—had departed from his primary source, Hall, in favour of Holinshed. He was, and one can be fairly confident about this, attracted by York's passion as a figure, or as an analogy of Christ's passion or, if not actually of Christ's passion, then of the representation of it in those

---

* But a producer might insist with equal likelihood on a "garland of sedges or bulrushes". In support of this kind of crown, see next page.

Mystery Cycles of the Middle Ages that were still being performed at this time or as recently, at least, as 1579. Especially does there seem to be here a direct or reported reminiscence—and not only because of the identity of personal and place names—of the pageants of the Buffeting and Crucifixion in the York Mystery Cycle. But, even without such a direct or indirect reminiscence on Shakespeare's part, that York's passion was a figure or analogy of Christ's is stated in Holinshed:

Some write that the duke was taken alive, and in derision caused to stand upon a molehill, on whose head they put a garland in steed of a crowne, which they had fashioned and made of sedges or bulrushes; and having so crowned him with that garland, they kneeled downe afore him (as the Jewes did unto Christ) in scorne, saieing to him: Haile king without rule, haile king without heritage, haile duke and prince without people or possessions . . .*

(whereas Hall, the main and only certain source for the play, apart from this scene of the death of York, reports that the 'crowning' took place after decapitation, and that the crown was made of "paper" and not of "sedges or bulrushes". Thus:

Yet this cruell Clifforde, & deadly bloudsupper not content with this homicyde, or chyldkillyng [i.e. of Rutland's killing] came to the place wher the dead corps of the duke of Yorke lay, and caused his head to be stryken of, and set on it a croune of paper, & so fixed it on a pole, & presented it to the Quene . . †).

It is evident that, for the death of York, Shakespeare preferred Holinshed to Hall, not because the former was thought of as a more reliable historian, but because Hall's account struck his imagination as being both more dramatic and more poetic: more dramatic, or more theatrical, negatively, because of the practical difficulty of beheading a player in view of the

* See G. Bullough: *Narrative and Dramatic Sources of Shakespeare*, vol. III, (Routledge & Kegan Paul, 1960), p. 210.

† *Ibid.*, p. 178. Professor Bullough notes that "In the play York is captured and Margaret puts the paper crown on his head before he is killed".

audience; more poetic—and dramatic—precisely because the enacting of the Holinshed version would promote, in the audience's mind, both memories of Christ's passion (as narrated in the Gospels) and of Christ's passion as re-enacted in the Mystery Cycles. Admittedly, Hall's comparison between the mock crowning, and the mock obeisance, rendered to York, and the mock crowning, and the mock obeisance, rendered to Jesus, is not *ex*plicitly made by Shakespeare, but *im*plicitly the resemblance between the suffering on the hill of Calvary and the suffering on the molehill on which York is planted is thrillingly transparent. Moreover, by choosing to follow Holinshed, rather than Hall, for this one episode the chance was offered to Shakespeare, which he accepted, of showing something of deep human interest, namely the spectacle of one member of a team of tormentors relucting at the excess of his companions, of bravely taking a stand in declaring that the 'fun' has gone far enough. Northumberland in *3 Henry VI* feels, as the First Servant in *King Lear*, when Gloster's remaining eye was to be pulled out, was to feel, that the torture applied to a human being, and to which he was at first a party, had gone far enough*.

Now, in the following scene of *3 Henry VI* (II. i.), the scene, which the audience has just witnessed as drama, is narrated by a Messenger. He tells York's sons, Edward and Richard:

> By many hands your Father was subdu'd,
> But onely slaught'red by the irefull Arme
> Of un-relenting Clifford, and the Queene:
> Who crown'd the gracious Duke in high despight,
> Laugh'd in his face: and when with griefe he wept,
> The ruthlesse Queene gave him, to dry his Cheekes,
> A Napkin, steeped in the harmelesse blood
> Of sweet young Rutland, by rough Clifford slaine:
> And after many scornes, many foule taunts,
> They tooke his Head, and on the Gates of Yorke

---

* At what point does the baiting of the deluded Malvolio go beyond the limits of Comedy, so that the Comedy becomes first uneasy, then wretched, then sour?

They set the same, and there it doth remaine,
The saddest spectacle that ere I view'd*.

II. i. 56–67

A possible attitude to this Interior Inset is that it is a reduplication of effort, is not even Plot-required. To the argument that it was necessary for the audience to see how York's sons took the news of their father's death, it might be answered that a Shakespeare, more experienced in the construction of plays, would have brought on York's sons in a mood of hardy defiance and revenge, having been informed *entre-d'acte*, as it were, of the manner of their father's death. They could, to improvise a pastiche, have entered with a

> O that oure Sire, of mighty York, the Duke,
> Should, like a lamb, at base-borne butcher's hands,
> Be done to death, and that a fiend of France
> Should, with traitorous hands, a crowne of reeds
> Sit on his haughty brow. But this I vow,
> Revenge shall sit . . . etc.,

or some such, and the scene would have had a lift at the start, would have dispensed with the Messenger as a 'character', and have spared the audience being told what they already knew.

But Shakespeare did not master this kind of economy, practical man of the theatre though he was, quickly. In a play of two or three years later, one which—whatever may be said of *3 Henry VI*—was wholly of his authorship, and which is almost as aesthetically flawless as anything he was later to achieve, *Romeo and Juliet*, we are presented in Act V with the spectacle of Friar Lawrence narrating to the assembled Montagues and Capulets (and the Prince of Verona) at extravagant length, though he says "I will be brief", what the audience have just been seeing, the deaths of Paris, Romeo and Juliet.

It might be urged that Shakespeare would have been hard put to it to suppose a way by which the leading citizens of

---

* The First Quarto (1595) adds the touch that York, when given the handkerchief, "weeping tooke it up". It also adds the lines
> Then through his brest they thrust their bloody swordes,
> Who like a lambe fell at the butchers feete,
which may allude to the paschal sacrifice as much as to the shambles at London, or at York, or everywhere.

Verona and its Prince could have been fully informed of the happenings in advance of their arrival at the graveyard—for the Watchman had babbled only a general alarm. Granting that the Montagues and the Capulets certainly had to be informed of something of which *they* could not have had previous knowledge (but which had just been shown to the audience), the Friar's narration also serves as an illustrated sermon. A feud between great families is destructive not only of civic peace, it can result in the deaths of the children of the feuding families, as witness this: and the gaze of two audiences follows in the direction of the Friar's. What the two audiences behold is an illustration to the Friar's story—a picture, or tableau, composed by the bodies of the children, Romeo and Juliet, and of Paris. The story is a sermon, albeit an unintended one, and its moral is pointed by *exempla horrenda*. The paying—or house—audience have watched the phases of composition of the tableau, is, in a measure, used to it, and now watch the reactions of the stage-audience (as it hears about the phases of the picture's composition) as well as following the focus of its gaze. In this way Shakespeare exploits a limiting necessity. The reduplicative effort points a moral.

Friar Lawrence's narration, with its visual illustration, is an Interior Plot-required Inset of special virtue. While the brief history, which is all "news" to the stage-audience, of the lovers is being narrated, the human *content* of the narration is presumably framed by the uprights and low horizontal of that supposed "inner stage" or "study" representing the mausoleum; moreover, all the while the narration is advancing the continuous "now" is also advancing so that the pathetic (or tragic) figures of the Friar's story are continuously being distanced by "ever mouing" time from the teller and his double audience*. Film-maker or television producer should

* This can be disputed, of course. Soon after the arrival of Montague on the scene, the Prince (in Fi) says, "Seale up the mouth of outrage for a while,/Till we can cleare these ambiguities". But there is no stage direction to indicate that the Prince's command is carried out, and the Friar's "Romeo *there* dead", fourteen lines later, rather suggests that the bodies remain open to view until the last line or so of the play. In the 1597 Quarto, the Prince's line reads, "Come seale your mouthes of outrage for a while" —a reproof to the bereaved parents, telling them to control their exclamations of grief until he's heard the Friar.

note that even in the theatre the figures of the dead Romeo and Juliet are retreating in time and visual focus and that, in their retreat, they transform, following the intention of the penitent and reconciled parents, to statues "of pure gold". The future takes over from present and past. Already, by the last line of the play, that image of two statues in the square of tourist-visited Verona begins to super-impose itself upon the picture of two corpses. There is a 'panning out' or distancing.

In the report by the Messenger in *3 Henry VI*, a less valuable and interesting effect is obtained. Yet the effect of the Messenger's lines is greater than the lines themselves deserve or would have obtained but for the directly preceding dramatizing of their substance. The paying audience, who are not virginal, for they have been exposed as Edward and Richard have not, to the action—*while it was happening*—have their memory revived. The (here) weak narrative poet is drawing on the capital which the dramatic poet had banked in the preceding scene. The paying audience will perceive or remember a more powerful image to accompany the lines than do the stage auditors, the image of one who, claiming to be King, was mocked and crowned on a dunghill. If the Messenger's narration does not enlarge that image it nevertheless preserves it from that dissolution to which most dramatic pictures in a rapidly moving chronicle play of this period are liable.

The Messenger's narration in *3 Henry VI* was an Inset of a kind that Shakespeare was to develop increasingly throughout his series of English History plays—back reference, a calling on accumulated capital, a borrowing on the past to give a fulness, a dignity, a perspective to an otherwise meagre present. In the Histories, a summoning to the memory of the past in order to give the otherwise sometimes paltry dramatic moment a vital power becomes increasingly a habit. Such a device may have been of practical service in refreshing the audience's memory under the pretext of informing stage auditors, but it also enabled Shakespeare to give frequently an otherwise flat 'here and now' a background, resonance and depth. Later, he was to apply the device, which he was called on to exercise in the construction of the early Chronicle plays, to those other *genres*—romantic comedy and tragedy.

2. OAK, MAN, SNAKE AND LIONESS

In *As You Like It*, IV. iii. the plot, derived from Lodge's
Rosalynde, requires that Oliver, eldest son of Sir Roland de
Boys, reappear in default of a *deus*. Oliver in II. ii. had been a
petty tyrant and a bully, a fairly powerfully wrought figure who
had set things in motion. He appears once only between I. i.
and IV. iii. In III. i., a brief scene, he is now the one to be
tyrannized and bullied—by Duke Fredericke. Where is his
brother? Oliver does not know, or care, and protests:

> Oh that your Highnesse knew my heart in this:
> I never lov'd my brother in my life.

This does not propitiate Fredericke:

> More villaine thou. Well push him out of dores
> And let my officers of such a nature
> Make an extent upon his house and Lands:
> Do this expediently, and turne him going.

Oliver, formidable in I. i., is rendered landless, homeless.
Evicted and helpless, he is nearly an object of pity; not quite
for he is now having a dose of his own medicine. 'Turn'd going',
he makes his way to Arden, has a misadventure which benefits
his soul so that he can now experience a natural affection for his
brother, and then, barbered and in "fresh array" comes on stage
in IV. iii., a redeemed character. Converted from hatred of
his brother to love of his brother, he will set half to rights. The
other half will be set to rights when the usurping Duke, who had
also been the "more villaine" for his brother-hatred, is also
"converted" and puts on "a Religious life".

It is a difficult part for an actor—that of Oliver de Boys. In
three widely spaced appearances he must impress as (*a*) an
imposing and ruthless landlord (whom a village Hampden
would do well to withstand), (*b*) the cringing victim of a more
powerful landlord, and (*c*) a morally reformed man and
romantic lover. The actor of Oliver, always one of mediocre
gifts, is not helped either by taking the same name 'Oliver' as
the ridiculous parson, Sir 'Oliver' Mar-Text. Shakespeare may
have been careless (or light-hearted) in *As You Like It* but, if so,
then the 'careless' duplication of names among the characters

in this play would interest a Freudian. The 'Oliver', that eldest brother and hedge-priest share, suggests that they might share more besides a name*.

By IV. iii. Oliver's existence has perhaps been forgotten by both audiences. If they need time to re-establish connections, to identify a changed character, they can do so while the new Oliver narrates a story about a "wretched ragged man", a she-snake and a lioness:

> Under an old Oake, whose bows were moss'd with age
> And high top, bald with drie antiquitie:
> A wretched ragged man, ore-growne with haire
> Lay sleeping on his back; about his necke
> A greene and guilded snake had wreath'd it selfe,
> Who with her head, nimble in threats approach'd
> The opening of his mouth: but sodainly
> Seeing Orlando, it unlink'd it selfe,
> And with indented glides, did slip away
> Into a bush, under which bushes shade
> A Lyonnesse, with udders all drawne drie,
> Lay cowching head on ground, with catlike watch
> When that the sleeping man should stirre: for 'tis
> The royall disposition of that beast
> To prey on nothing, that doth seeme as dead:
> This seene, Orlando did approach the man,
> And found it was his brother, his elder brother.

Until the last of these lines (with the later confirmation 'I am that brother'), the two audiences can divide their attention between conjecturing the identity of the intruder and apprehending the Inset picture the intruder creates. Oliver's narrative 'gangs up'† some of Shakespeare's most powerful images, thus

> A wretched ragged man, ore-growne with haire

connects with the "Hedges . . ./Like Prisoners wildly overgrowne with hayre" in Burgundy's speech in *Henry V*, V. ii., a play of about the same date as *As You Like It*, and the "old Oake, whose bows were moss'd with age" looks forward to the

---

* And there are two 'Jacques' as well as two 'Olivers'.

† I have in mind E. A. Armstrong's account of image clusters in his *Shakespeare's Imagination*.

"moyst Trees,/That have outliv'd the Eagle" in *Timon of Athens*, IV. iii.*. Still, it must be accepted that the narrative lacks the intensity of Shakespeare's greatest poetry (the "old", "with age", "drie antiquitie" are repeats rather than increments), though it is one of the more powerful passages in *As You Like It*.

Lodge in *Rosalynde* has presented the episode thus:

All this while did poore *Saladyne* [Shakespeare's Oliver] (Banished from *Bourdeaux* and the Court of *France* by *Torismond*) [Duke Fredericke], wander up and downe in the Forrest of *Arden*, thinking to get to *Lions*, and so travell through *Germanie* into *Italy*: but the Forrest being full of by-pathes, and he unskilfull of the Countrey coast, slipt out of the way, and chaunced up into the Desart, not farre from the place where *Gerismond* [Duke Senior] was, and his brother *Rosader* [Orlando]. *Saladyne* wearie with wandring up and downe, and hungrie with long fasting; finding a little cave by the side of a thicket, eating such frute as the Forrest did affoord, and contenting himselfe with such drinke as Nature had provided and, thirst made delicate, after his repast he fell in a dead sleepe. As thus he lay, a hungrie Lion came hunting downe the edge of the grove for pray, and espying *Saladyne* began to ceaze upon him: but seeing he lay still without anie motion, he left to touch him, for that Lions hate to pray on dead carkasses: and yet desirous to have some foode, the Lion lay down and watcht to see if hee would stirre†.

Contrasted with his handling of North's description of Cleopatra in her barge, Shakespeare—in the operation of translating prose into verse—here altered and added. Thus Oliver is shaggy like a prisoner, or an unpruned hedge in France during wartime, and he falls asleep under an ancient oak and not inside a cave; Lodge's lion is changed into a lioness; a vividly realized snake is introduced—female, like the lioness, though how the

---

* Warburton amended "moyst" to "moss'd". Walter Whiter in his *Specimen Commentary* (1797) argued brilliantly for the authority of the Folio reading given here. Nevertheless most editors have followed Warburton. 'Oaks' in Shakespeare—as in Jonson—are usually ancient (e.g. "the un-wedgable and gnarled Oke" of *Measure for Measure*). But why should the "Trees that have outliv'd the Eagle" be oaks in *Timon*? Because they have outlived the longevitous eagle and in their "drie antiquitie" are mossed, not moist, and (perhaps) because 'oak' occurs twice elsewhere in the same scene.

† *Narrative and Dramatic Sources of Shakespeare*, Vol. II, p. 215.

snake's sex could be deduced by Orlando so rapidly and in such critical circumstances is beyond guessing. In life it is doubtful whether a zoologist would have known its sex; but this "greene and guilded snake" exists not in life but in imagination, and in the laws of the imagination it is, though indefinably (except by recourse to psychology) *right* that the beautiful and baneful creature in the picture—terrifying as a snake in a dream*— wreathed around the sleeper's neck and about to dart its head into his mouth, should have been female, just as it is right that the serpent that seduced Eve should have been male.

Why the Lodge lion into the Shakespeare lioness? Possibly because Lodge's Saladyne was trying to get to Lyons ("Lions") and as the lion encountered Saladyne so the 's' of the place-name encountered Shakespeare†. Further, a lioness, with cubs, is more ferocious than the lion; its exercise of motherhood allows of development in the picture; in her sex she is in league with the snake against the unbarbered man sleeping under the oak; the bloodied napkin, the work of the lioness, startles Ganimed into betraying her true sex by her fainting (*Oliver:* "You a man? You lacke a mans heart. *Rosilind:* I doe so, I confesse it."); and this comedy, like others, is a war between the sexes: Oliver is rescued from she-snake and lioness to fall victim to Aliena; lioness-mauled Orlando to fall victim to a man-ess, Ganimed-Rosalind. The theatre-audience knows more about the realities and the possibilities than does Oliver's stage-audience consisting of the disguised Rosalind and Celia; but, from the point of view (literally) of either audience, the Inset picture is functionally involved in the play that contains it. Apart from eliciting the sissyness of Ganimed, when confronted by blood, it narrates what could not be shown any more than Ophelia's drowning could be shown for "to bring in

* Cp. Hermia's dream in *Midsummer Night's Dream*, II. ii.:
  Helpe me Lysander, helpe me; do thy best
  To plucke this crawling serpent from my brest.
  Aye me, for pitty; what a dreame was here?
Oliver would have seen the lioness in battle with Orlando; unless he *also* dreamed about the snake while it was engaged on him, his brilliant description of it, and its movements, must have been derived from Orlando.

† Neither a lion nor a lioness likely in Arden or the Ardennes; but more acceptable as possible, in the gradation series of belief, after the likely and convincing snake.

(God shield us) a Lyon among Ladis, is a most dreadfull thing"; nor would a tame snake be all that tractable in rehearsal.

Oliver has a nearly major poem to narrate. His stage-audience have to be attentive and static until Ganimed swoons. At that point the imaged and the physically real pictures coalesce; *until* that point the theatre-audience is given time to accommodate itself to the idea of a complete character change in the Oliver of I. i. and in the Oliver of III. i. by concentrating not on him but on the Inset picture composed of mossed oak, sleeping unbarbered man, snake and lioness—a picture rendered in such vivid detail that it could be actually painted, as no doubt it has been.

3. CARDINAL BLEMISH

In *3 Henry VI* an event is first shown and then narrated; another instance of this occurs in *Cymbeline*; i.e. the one and the same event is viewed at different perspectives in—and of—time and presented from different technical approaches. In Act II. sc. ii. Iachimo, having issued 'from the Trunke', contemplates the sleeping Imogen, makes an inventory of the furnishings of her bed-chamber, removes a bracelet from her arm, (presumably) takes off her bed-clothes to record "some naturall notes about her Body",

> On her left brest
> A mole Cinque-spotted: Like the Crimson drops
> I'th'bottome of a Cowslippe,

and then gets into the trunk again, pulling the lid down, as the clock strikes three. Two scenes later, Iachimo is in Philario's house in Rome, where he gives Posthumus a true—or approximately true*—account of the observations he had made in

---

* True, or approximately true. The only lie in Iachimo's report is when, speaking about the bracelet, he says "She stript it from her Arme" whereas *he* stripped it from *her* arm. 'The only lie' because when he swears ("By my life") that he kissed the mole there is no-one to say that he didn't, and he probably did (or should do in a production) between "Cowslippe" and "Heere's a Voucher". It is obvious that Iachimo's prayer to "sleepe, thou Ape of death" is answered, and that it does "lye dull upon her". It is also clear that Iachimo had earlier kissed Imogen's lips *once*: "one kisse. Rubies unparagon'd,/How deerely they doo't".

(and of) Imogen's "Bed-chamber", produces the evidence of
the bracelet, and finally convinces the husband that he had
"tasted her in Bed" by telling him about "some corporall signe
about her"—the mole (it is unnecessary now to specify whether
left or right breast). Iachimo says:

> under her Breast
> (Worthy her pressing) lyes a Mole, right proud
> Of that most delicate Lodging. By my life
> I kist it, and it gave me present hunger
> To feede againe, though full.

Posthumus, convinced by this, arranges for his 'false' wife to be
killed. Now what is remarkable about the dramatic showing in
II. ii. and its narrative duplication in II. iv. is that it is the
dramatic II. ii. which has rather the properties of the narrative
Inset and the narrative II. iv. which has the properties of the
foreground dramatic. This is partly by reason that II. ii. is a
Iachimo monologue (he is informing the theatre-audience
and not an unconscious Imogen—that is, he is not *en rapport*
with any stage personage) while II. iv. is a duologue between
Iachimo and Posthumus, wherein what Iachimo narrates of the
past by instalments (since Posthumus interrogates, interrupts,
explains away) becomes of immediate present importance
(how will—does—should—Posthumus react?), but only partly.
Additionally, the dramatic appears narrative and the narrative
dramatic because of the deposition of figures and forces (and
properties), in both scenes, on the Elizabethan stage.

The Folio stage-direction for II. ii. is "Enter Imogen, in her
Bed, and a Lady". This points to the scene being a discovery
scene; indeed, it is inconceivable how the bed and its occupant
—who with her opening lines makes it clear that she has been
lying in bed and reading for three hours*—could be presented
except by discovery. The curtains of the lower inner-stage or of

---

* *Imogen:* Who's there? My woman: Helene?
  Lady: Please you Madam.
  Imogen: What houre is it?
  Lady: Almost midnight, Madam.
  Imogen: I have read three houres then.

In a moment she is asleep. Iachimo is accordingly out of the trunk for three
hours. No scene in Shakespeare offers clearer evidence for the existence of
an inner-stage in his theatre.

the upper inner-stage (behind the tarras) are drawn back to disclose the 'set' of Imogen's bed-chamber, a 'set' decorated by the "Arras" and equipped with the burning "Taper" and the "Such, and such pictures" that Iachimo registers in his notebook. When Iachimo has returned to his trunk and pulled the lid down, the curtains are drawn to mask the inner-stage in preparation for Cloten's *aubade* in the next scene. At whatever the level—main platform level or tarras level—it is patent, from all we know of the Elizabethan theatre and of theatrical production, that II. ii. is played in an alcove, at long distance from the audience. Moreover, it is only on the assumption of such a long perspective that Iachimo's stripping of the bed-coverings and inspection of Imogen's body would be practicable, whichever the sex of the player of Imogen. The 'dramatic' II. ii. is played up-stage in an alcove while the 'narrative' II.iv., where Iachimo reports his adventure, and truthfully except as to how he came by the bracelet, is equally clearly played *down*—close to the audience. It is this *crossing* of visual and auditory effects, this countering of literary *genre* by pictorial perspective, this transposing of the usual relation between word and picture, that is responsible for the derangement. It is the dramatic II. ii. which produces the Inset picture in defiance of tense inflections; it is the narrative II. iv. which is dramatic since its foreground presentation underlines Posthumus' *present* reactions despite Iachimo's *past* tense.

Yet the Inset effect of II. ii. is not entirely due to the pictorial reality—for the scene literally takes place in an 'Inset'. Whatever the tense of Iachimo's monologue, it is a monologue that he utters. This means that if Iachimo assumes any audience it is certainly not Imogen (may *she* not hear, may she remain safely unconscious). If Iachimo assumes any audience at all it is the theatre-audience who are allowed to *over*hear. The tone, pace, rhythm, pitch and volume of his speech, though in the dramatic tense, are—at the outset—those of the narrative or of the reflective lyric:

> The Crickets sing, and mans ore-labor'd sense
> Repaires it selfe by rest: Our Tarquine thus
> Did softly presse the Rushes, ere he waken'd
> The Chastitie he wounded.

And if it be questioned whether these low-voiced accents could reach the distant audience, it must be confessed they could because of the resonantal qualities of the box or alcove where they are spoken. Though there are reminiscences of both *Macbeth* ("With *Tarquins* ravishing strides, towards his designe/ Moves like a Ghost") and *Lucrece*, the movement of this verse is more like the movement of the verse of the narrative*, except for those phrases where he signals his business, e.g. "But my designe . . . I will write all downe", or except for those questions which he formally puts to himself in lieu of a stage-audience ("No more: to what end?/Why should I write this downe, that's riveted,/Screw'd to my memorie") and except that the speech quickens in urgency with the completion of his task:

> Swift, swift, you Dragons of the night, that dawning
> May bare the Ravens eye: I lodge in feare,
> Though this a heavenly Angell: hell is heere.
>   *Clock strikes*
> One, two, three: time, time.

If Imogen had woken up, as Lucrece and Desdemona had woken up, and had held discourse with the intruder, the scene would have been instantly 'forwarded' into the focus and idiom of drama; but since she does not wake up, and since Iachimo's addresses to her ("fresh Lilly") and to "sleepe" are alike apostrophic, the scene—which of course is one of the most superb things in Shakespeare—remains remote. The whole unoccupied space of the main platform stage intervenes between the spectators and the single conscious creature in the alcove whose activity is nearly limited to describing its contents. Description is the principal organ of the narrative art. The Inset scene completed, the main stage is promptly alive with the busy 'forward' action of Cloten's *aubade*, the entry of Cymbeline and the Queen, Cloten's knocking at the door of Imogen's house (the postern beside the inner-stage) and the entry of first

* Shakespeare's reminiscence of *Lucrece* in these scenes of *Cymbeline* is strong. In both works are "Lilly" and "Monument"; in both the 'eyes', 'breast' and 'Arras hangings'—though the subject of the *Lucrece* tapestry is the sack of Troy and the subject of the *Cymbeline* tapestry is of "Proud Cleopatra, when she met her Roman,/And Sidnus swell'd above the Bankes" (II. iv.).

Imogen's Lady and then Imogen herself. The preceding
scene is now firmly cordoned off as an Inset, a memory to be
revived in II. iv.

Iachimo's narrative begins briskly:

> First, her Bed-chamber
> (Where I confesse I slept not, but professe
> Had that was well worth watching) it was hang'd
> With Tapistry of Silke, and Silver, the Story
> Proud Cleopatra, when she met her Roman,
> And Sidnus swell'd above the Bankes, or for
> The presse of Boates, or Pride. A peece of Worke
> So bravely done, so rich, that it did strive
> In Workemanship, and Value, which I wonder'd
> Could be so rarely, and exactly wrought
> Since the true life on't was—
>
> *Posthumus:* This is true:
> And this you might have heard of heere, by me,
> Or by some other.
>
> *Iachimo:* More particulars
> Must justifie my knowledge.
>
> *Posthumus:* So they must,
> Or . . .*

Brisk is Iachimo's narrative in the past tense and brisk are
Posthumus' interruptions in the tone, tense ("is") and temper
of the here and now. This is undeniably front-of-the-platform
dialogue exchange, and it leads up to a forthright culminating
'here and now'—or dramatic—passion after Iachimo has
detailed the "corporall signe" about Imogen. It is interesting
then to note that the tense that Iachimo employs when he
comes to specify the "signe" is the present "lyes". Of course it
"lyes", but equally currently *existing* are the figures of the
tapestry and the "Chimney-peece" showing "Chaste Dian,
bathing". Yet the meeting of Antony and Cleopatra is reported

---

* Various verbal and thematic preoccupations of Shakespeare's converge
in these two scenes of *Cymbeline*. Presumably they released a number of
memory streams which had flowed in *Lucrece*, *Macbeth* and *Antony and
Cleopatra*. The 'co-adunative' (Coleridge's term) word would seem to be
'press' and its inflections. Thus Iachimo moves like Tarquin, "Our Tarquine
thus/Did softly *presse* the Rushes"; thus "The *presse* of Boates" may have
raised the level of the Cydnus in the tapestry; thus Imogen's left breast was
"Worthy her *pressing*".

as perfected, and, as for "the Cutter" of the chimney-piece, he "*was*" and he "out-*went*":

> the Cutter
> Was an another Nature dumbe, out-went her,
> Motion and Breath left out.

Iachimo keeps to the past tense when describing the artifacts in Imogen's bed-chamber: he keeps to that tense when he says that not he, but Imogen, plucked off the bracelet which he now shows:

> She stript it from her Arme: I see her yet:
> Her pretty Action, did out-sell her guift,
> And yet enrich'd it too: she gave it me,
> And said, she priz'd it once.

and Posthumus remains in control. If Iachimo had said "lay" the result might have been different, but it is the "lyes" in

> If you seeke
> For further satisfying, under her Breast
> (Worthy her pressing) *lyes* a Mole, right proud
> Of that most delicate Lodging. By my life
> I kist it . . .

which drives Posthumus wild. Nor is it, I think, fanciful to note that the diphthong in "l*ye*s" is accentuated (or rubbed in) by that identical diphthong in "satisf*y*ing", "r*i*ght", "l*i*fe", "*I*". It wrings out of Posthumus, as his first sound of surrender on conviction, 'I':

> *I* [*i.e. aye*], and it doth confirme
> Another staine . . .

which he follows with

> If you will sweare you have not done't, you *lye*,
> And *I* will kill thee, if thou do'st den*y*
> Thou'st made me Cuckold.

In II. iv. the theatre-audience is given a minutely detailed account of the tapestry, the chimney-piece, the roof and the andirons of Imogen's bed-chamber which it is not given in II. ii. for the reason that these furnishings would have been physically too far distant for the audience to check (or the playhouse did not have properties to correspond with the later description, or, if they had, the correspondence would have provoked a heinous distraction from the *then* important). Apart from this consideration, it is amusing to note that by 1610 or 1611 Shakespeare was easily able to work transverse effects—to endow the dramatic mode with an Inset power by positioning it in the background and to endow the narrative mode with dramatic immediacy by placing it in the foreground. This is a counterpointing of word and picture, and it is more than a matter of expertise: Shakespeare in these two scenes of *Cymbeline* is offering different approaches to a still 'pressing' event in his actual, imagined, or reading, memory.

*   *   *

The Interior Plot-required Inset, whether or not it duplicated an event previously shown, afforded opportunities to the narrative poet to focus on minute detail, to present 'cinematographic' close-ups to the imaginative vision, e.g. Imogen's cardinal blemish, or physically unseeable and unactable movements. It allowed Shakespeare to realize in poetry the life of animals which it would be inexpedient, or impossible, to expose on the stage. As he had been free to realize the life of Poor Wat, the hare, and the breeding jennet in *Lucrece*, so he became free to realize a palfrey in *Richard II* or a snake in *As You Like It*. Besides a reserve of physically invisible actors, divine, human (dead in *The Winter's Tale*) and animals, it enabled him to call in such natural adjuncts as a river or a cliff.

On each occasion that this Inset occurs it reveals, on examination, that the imprisonment imposed on a dramatic poet has provoked the freedom of the narrative artist.

V. The Voluntary Inset

To be distinguished from (i) the Expository Inset (the Inset which has the necessary, but mechanical, task of narrating information concerning the history of the characters without which the audience could not understand the action of the play now to be shown), and from (ii) the Interior Plot-required Inset (which also has a necessary, but mechanical, task, that of narrating an episode, supposed to have occurred within the time span of the presented action, either because it cannot be shown or because the poet prefers to tell it rather than to show it), is that kind of Inset which is, in a sense, gratuitous. It is gratuitous in that it is not required by the plot. This kind of Inset, which I therefore call the Voluntary, is unnecessary or expendable in that a narrative of this kind could be 'cut' from a text during its performance without the audience being any, or scarcely any, the worse as to their understanding of the plot—as to their knowing what's going on. A Voluntary Inset contributes in a way other than an 'advance of the action': indeed it can fairly seem to effectually 'delay the action'. All Insets, it could be objected, hold up the action in that stage-movement (with "the action suited to the word, the word to the action") is arrested *while* a time (other than the stage 'now') and *while* a place (other than the stage 'here') are evoked in a narrative poem. That is so, but the Voluntary Inset interrupts not merely the stage-movement—in the manner of other kinds of Inset—but, apparently, at least, the Aristotelean action also. For, though the Expository and the Interior Plot-required Insets hold up stage-movement, the audience is meanwhile at any rate given information (during that suspension) which will enable them to understand the stage-movement the better when it is resumed. With the Voluntary it is otherwise: it does not either directly, as when the theatre-audience is addressed, or indirectly, as when the theatre-audience is addressed through a stage-auditor, offer information useful for an understanding of the plot or, if it does offer a few grains, that is an incidental yield. On the other hand, a Voluntary Inset can, and often does, yield information—whether this is its primary function or merely a side effect remains to be investigated—which adds to the audience's understanding of the *character* who narrates it by revealing aspects of that character which are suppressed when it is wholly engaged in dialogue dedicated to furthering the here-and-now of the existing situation. Hence a Voluntary Inset can add to the audience's perception of the whole of a play despite the temporary suspension of physical movement which it inflicts. Only in a crude sense of the word, or only when a stage-production is under the control of an insensitive director, is a Voluntary Inset expendable. Nevertheless, Shakespeare practised this, his most interesting kind of Inset, with degrees of success.

I. THE PINING STATUE

For our first example of the Voluntary we choose Viola's lie about a sister who died from unrequited love (*Twelfth Night*, II. iv.). She tells a whopping lie—for we accept this 'sister' to be fictional, that she is a cover, or hide, from behind which she expresses her own hopeless love for Orsino—in a passage which reverberates in the minds of hearers and spectators as the most poignant in the play, if not in all Shakespeare. Indeed, this Inset—where the two characters concerned are utterly static as one of them, in a narrative poem, draws on memory or invention to evoke a place and time remote (apparently) from the theatre-audience's, and even the play's interests— which could be omitted altogether from a production in the theatre with negligible loss to an understanding of the plot— not only lingers in the memory but can eventually convince that it is in here, precisely, in this Inset, that the essence of *Twelfth Night* abides. What was an expendable narrative poem, placed in a drama and holding up its advance, becomes, if not immediately then on recollection, the centre of *Twelfth Night* and the enshrinement of its action*.

How is this effect obtained?

In II. iv., after Orsino and Viola-Cesario, Curio and other attendants, have been entertained by the Clown's Song ('entertained', but the love-longing of two of the Clown's auditors has been stimulated rather than soothed by the song), Orsino dismisses ("Let all the rest give place") everyone except his 'page'. Orsino then returns to his charge,

> Get thee to yond same soveraigne crueltie . . .

To Viola-Cesario's objections that the mission will be in vain, that Olivia's constitution, her temperament, prevent her fastening her affections on Orsino; that love is not obedient to the elective will but to the affective will; that she will not love him even if she would because "she cannot", Orsino is resistant, declaring that he "cannot so be answer'd". But the 'boy' Cesario, who had earlier in the scene revealed that he was a scholar of the heart, as one who had spoken "masterly" on the nature of love, replies that his (her) lord can do nothing but submit to the fact that amorous craving can be one-sided, and he (she) illustrates the truth by the supposition that "some Lady" feels for Orsino as Orsino feels for Olivia, likewise in vain, equally without return. Orsino declares that Cesario's supposition is false for the scientific reason that the sheer physical construction of women is other—and weaker—than the physical construction of men, that they would be anatomically incapable of sustaining the passion of love in any degree comparable to that which men can conceive or tolerate. Surely the 'boy' should know that? The 'boy' perhaps knows this but the woman—Viola—denies it, the audience perhaps

---

* It is no part of my argument that Shakespeare should create a Voluntary Inset independent of all suggestions from his actual or possible sources. Shakespeare "may have known *Gl'Inganni* and *L'Interesse* of Nicolò Secchi . . . Each contains a brief passage in which the disguised heroine tells of a fictitious lady". (G. Bullough, *Narrative and Dramatic Sources of Shakespeare*, Vol. II, p. 274.) Bullough refers, in a footnote, to H. A. Kaufman, 'Nicolò Secchi as a source of *Twelfth Night*', *Sh.Q.* 5, 1954, 271–280, and to her edition of a translation of *L'Interesse*. Similarly, Bandello, or his translator Belleforest, may have provided Shakespeare with hints for Viola's lie.

realizing that, whether he is right or wrong in his argument from anatomy, that Orsino has not met Cesario's case (which is that a woman can love without return) by replying not that they don't love, but that they cannot love as strongly as men*.

Cesario, however, denies the proposition that women cannot suffer love as intensely as men, because they are physically weaker, since he "knows" to the contrary. "What does he know?" Well, he knows that women are "as true", if not as strong, "of heart" as men and that therefore they can, because they are weaker, pine away—their longing unreturned—to death. He has evidence of the accuracy of this statement. And what is that evidence? The evidence is a lie. The speaker never had a sister; 'he' invents one to serve *her* turn, to illustrate *his* contention or, as we said, as a cover from behind which 'she' admits her own crisis *through* her stage-auditor, Orsino, to the theatre-audience. Alternatively, it might be pleaded, that Cesario-Viola is not so much deceiving his stage-listener as deceiving herself, and that innocently; that this 'sister' is a phantasy sister, an eidolon on and into whom 'he' bestows all her concealed femininity—that is, her incontestable reality beneath the "masculine usurp'd attyre" of the Page. Cesario-Viola is of course a profoundly ambiguous figure—she is a 'he' to Orsino, he is a 'she' to the paying audience. Her disguise, like all disguise, is there to deceive, but transvestism *this way round* is a rich and enchanting thing in Shakespeare†. Hence, although the words 'lie' and 'deception' have been strictly enough used, with respect to this Inset, it is realized that no moral verdict is pronounced or even involved. Moral issues can be involved in a Shakespeare romantic comedy (in *Twelfth Night* we feel the passion with which Antonio charges the supposed Sebastian with ingratitude and would grant its justice if Viola had been Sebastian; we feel, in the cause of

* It is only too likely that many of the audience do *not* realize that Orsino has not answered an argument but merely shifted his ground, that he has produced a "red herring", because they often conduct an argument in a similar way themselves.

† *The other way round* is a very different matter, ludicrous and undignified. The one stage appearance, in Shakespeare, is Falstaff's as the Fat Woman of Brainford (*Merry Wives*, IV. ii.). Antony and Cleopatra refer to their exchange of clothing, but Antony is not shown in Cleopatra's garb, and the exchange was an act of amatory sportiveness.

compassion, that the ragging of Malvolio goes too far, etc.), but they are not involved in the scene under discussion. In this scene morals and morality are less disregarded than transcended. And why? Antonio and Malvolio feel injured or *ab*used; no-one is being injured because of Viola's deceiving garments or her lying narrative. That is a practical explanation. A better one would be—no disguise and no mistakes through a disguise, no Comedy. Better still: Cesario's ill-fated 'sister' springs from the speaker's deepest dreads *and* desires. So do our dreams, and our dreams are beyond moral censure because they are created from depths of personality beyond the control of the moral will. If this is true of the scene as a whole, it is more positively true of the Voluntary Inset which the scene contains and which is its arcanum.

To return to that Inset. Orsino demands, "What dost thou know?", to Cesario's reply that he/she "knows" something which refutes, utterly refutes, Orsino's assertion, claimed to be based on anatomical facts, that no woman "can" love to the same degree as men. Cesario knows

> Too well what love women to men may owe,

"too well", and she has her evidence in the shape of the "history" of her fake sister to adduce in support.

And so Orsino's question, "And what's her history?"

Up to this point there has been a complete coherence between Word and Picture; between what the audience hear and what the audience (as spectators) see; the "action has been suited to the word, the word to the action"—action in the sense of disposition of figures on the stage, their stance, their gestures. The time is now, the place is here. The discussion between Duke and Page has arisen out of the Duke's request to Cesario to undertake another embassy to Olivia, necessary for furthering the main plot, and the discussion itself has centred on the unlikelihood of the coming embassy's success because of the nature of Olivia, of women, and of love. But when Cesario narrates the "history" of her sister, the coherence between stage picture and language is dissolved, for the audience's imaginative vision is as much captured by the figure seated "like Patience on a Monument" as their physical vision is retained by the two figures on the stage. As for the figures on the stage—they become, in the argot of the theatrical producer, 'frozen'; all movements by the seated auditor and standing narrator must become, as it were, hushed. The stage-picture becomes static, exerts merely a bare retaining authority, as we are led from the here (of Orsino's palace in Illyria) and the now (of the moment in the progress of the plot) to another time and another place, to a *there* and a *then* which is at variance with what the audience physically behold and what they have been beholding.

Another time, another place. What time? What place? That other time and place are not the temporal and local setting of an event anterior to, but casually connected with, 'the story of the play', as is the Sea Captain's account of how he saw Sebastian "binde himselfe/... To a strong Maste, that liv'd upon the sea" (II. i.), nor are they the setting of an event causally connected with the plot, occurring within its temporal span, but which Shakespeare could not show or preferred not to show. The Inset in II. iv. is neither expository nor plot-required in function and the time and the place of Cesario's narrative are of an order different from those obtaining in Expository and Interior Plot-required Insets. The *there* of the Voluntary Inset in *Twelfth Night*, II. iv. is free of any connection with the scene of the play and the *then* is free of any connection with the chronology of the play's action. But since the figure of the sister created in these lines is of doubtful historicity, is rather an eidolon—a projection of the speaker's own concealed yearning—that the dimensions of time and place in which she (or it) exists should be equally independent of actuality is not surprising.

And what's her history?

Viola: A blanke my Lord: she never told her love,
But let concealment like a worme i'th' budde
Feede on her damaske cheeke; she pin'd in thought,
And with a greene and yellow melancholly,
She sate like Patience on a Monument,
Smiling at greefe . . .

The doubt as to the historicity of Viola's sister, her indeterminacy in actual time, despite the containing past indicative, "My Father *had* a daughter *lov'd* a man", makes it difficult to assert whether the visionary Inset picture (of a girl freezing into an immobility—"like Patience on a Monument"—even more absolute than the immobility of the two figures composing the stage picture) is—or seems to be—nearer to, or further from, the audience than the physically visible stage-picture. Usually, where the substance of a Shakespearean Inset relates to the real historical past of a character, the Inset picture seems to be positively placed in remoter perspective than the stage picture—the temporal recession requiring an accompanying pictorial recession. Indeed, in the final plays, where Dumb Shows illustrate a retrospective narrative, it can be inferred from the text—the inference borne out by modern theatrical practice—that the illustrations must take place up-stage*.

Here it is difficult, not because the distance between the audience and the stage picture is measurable, while the distance between audience and their visionary picture is, though none the less real, immeasurable, but because the figure of a human girl seated "like Patience on a Monument", though conveyed as a historic fact ("My Father had a daughter"), is equally speculative and possible as real and past. The figure is as much an image of Cesario's fears for her future *as Viola* as it is of the sister's grief in the past. The doubt about the historicity of the sister, then, prevents us from distancing the picture, of which she is the centre, into the background of the actually visible scene as we distance, for instance, the picture of Hamlet Senior "When in an angry parle/He smote the sledded Polack on the ice", for what is remote in time is remote in space. But the temporal *ambivalence* of the figure in the picture evoked in Cesario's narrative, since she (or it) is as much an image of emerging possibility in the future as a past fact, is paralleled by a visual ambivalence: the fictive sister's history is equally Viola's possible fate. Hence the visionary picture is as much obtrusive as recessive in relation to the stage-picture. Indeed, we may feel that its dimensions come to correspond with the dimensions of the stage-picture. We suspect that the stage-picture is not only totally filled by the visionary picture, but is subdued by it while it

* See pp. 149–150 below.

lasts. The stage-picture, with its two static figures—lay figures for the persons of the narrative—simply retains enough physical reality and authority to act as a frame for the visionary picture which floods it.

The stage-picture has two figures (or three in the sense that Cesario is two persons in one); the picture of the Voluntary Inset has two figures (that of the sister and that of the man she loved) becoming but a single one—and that single one more like the loneliest of statues than a living girl—in the end. There is this congruence between the two pictures: the girl, who gradually became "like Patience on a Monument", is, by the end of the narrative, as still and silent as the narrator and listener on the stage, until the visionary picture is broken by Viola's "Sir, shall I to this Lady?"

With Cesario's "Sir, shall I to this Lady?" and the Duke's reply, "I that's the theame", there is of course a dissolution, if not a dismissal, of the Inset. What had occluded the stage-picture (though it is remembered) vanishes; business returns; time returns to the *now*, the place returns to the *here*; the suspended plot is resumed; the Duke and his Page are freed to move. All this is accompanied by a vocal change, the resumption of a style of vocal delivery adjusted to a continuing and developing 'here' and 'now', the vocal inflexions expressive of current decisions being made in the confidence that they will determine the future.

For it will be noticed that during the Voluntary Inset the player of Cesario-Viola is obliged to adopt (it is not a matter of deliberation or histrionic expertise) a mode of delivery appropriate to nostalgic reminiscence, appropriate to utterance of matter dependent on "had", the grammatical inflexion of the past tense.

In the speaking of the three lines

> My Father had a daughter lov'd a man
> As it might be perhaps, were I a woman
> I should your Lordship,

there should obviously be a vocal differentiation between the first line, which states a past fact in the perfect indicative (that the fact is highly questionable we know but the first audience— at *this* point—did not) and its two successors which exquisitely and coyly (they are presumably uttered with a side-long glance) hint at an engaging impossibility (to the stage-auditor) or possibility (to the theatre audience) in the subjunctive mood. Against the "had" of line 1, the "might be", the "were I" and the "I should" of lines 2 and 3 vibrate. And though the grammatical inflexions lie—for it is the first line which is hypothetical, the second and third which state the indicative fact—the lies are no lies to the stage-auditor. The theatre audience, admittedly, view and listen otherwise, but—for all the talk of 'dramatic irony'—are not so destructively omniscient as all that: they see and hear as much 'with' Orsino as 'with' a 'Viola' who is even more attractive as a 'Cesario'. Stage- and theatre-audience alike weigh the differences of pitch (line 1 low; lines 2 and 3 rising), pace (line 1 slow; lines 2 and 3 quickening*) and timbre (line 1 grave—it is reminiscent, what's done is done, the 'sister' is dead; lines 2 and 3 mellow—they insinuate and toss in the air a hypothesis at once impossible to the stage-auditor and more than possible—the desired truth awaiting disclosure and consummation—to the theatre-audience). The theatre-audience weighs, consciously or not, the difference between the tone (granting to 'tone' a summarization of all these vocal qualities) appropriate to an Inset—relating to a time and place distinct from those manifest in, and declared by, the stage-picture—from the tone appropriate to a current dramatic situation which is impelled to grow into another.

But Orsino takes up not the 'real impossibility' but the 'impossible reality' with his "And what's her history?" and thus invites the narrator to resume the tense and tone of line 1. This leads into her Voluntary Inset which, although from one aspect it has little to do with the plot, leads into the very heart of the play—however much at variance that heart may be to the literal scene before the spectators.

And what's her history? Orsino neglects the subjunctive possibility; either out of tact, or because he is already lured into the past, he takes up the pseudo-factual statement instead and thus encourages Cesario—he needed little persuasion—to

---

* But with shy and subtle pauses, accompanied by shy and subtle side-long glances. She ought to blush at the daring of the hypothesis.

relate that history:

> A blanke my Lord: she never told her love
> But let concealment like a worme i'th' budde
> Feede on her damaske cheeke: she pin'd in thought,
> And with a greene and yellow melancholly,
> She sat like Patience on a Monument,
> Smiling at greefe.

The verbal inflexions, 'told', 'feede', 'pin'd', place the pathetic 'history' as a perfected action. The theatre-audience know otherwise; they know that the suppressed Viola is figuring her probable future; but the stage-auditor, ignorant of the presence of the mammalia under the Page's doublet, and ignorant that the codpiece is a stuffed dummy, is deceived by the verbal inflexions into believing that Cesario is narrating a real and—since he learns that the sister is dead—irrecoverable past*. Now anyone, narrating a perfected action, adopts the appropriate tone.

The tone is as difficult to define. For here it is not simply an ineluctable slice of history (or pseudo-history) that is being told. Some New England poet declares that the saddest of expressions is "might have been". The point of Cesario's history is 'it might have been otherwise', the 'sister's' love *might have been* requited. The past indicative verbs of Cesario's narrative contain a 'might have been'; the sister would not have 'pin'd' *if* . . . . This explains the pathos. It is not merely a tale of the irredeemable past, the love yearning was 'hopeless' even when that past was present. (The suppressed Viola's passion is not 'hopeless', as the theatre-audience knows, and suspects that 'she' suspects—after all Olivia "cannot" love at will and Cesario *has* certain goods under her doublet and inside her hose which she is keeping up her sleeve, so to speak.)

It is this factual narrative of a *might have been*, framed in a past that is accepted by the stage-auditor as real ("My Father *had* a daughter"), that compels on the part of Cesario-Viola the

---

* The stage-auditor, Orsino, is 'ignorant' within the terms of the play in which he and Cesario are characters; the theatre-audience know that 'Cesario' is Viola and that the part of Viola is played by a boy. The whole matter of transvestism and bi-sexuality in drama is illuminated by G. Wilson Knight in his *The Golden Labyrinth*, 1962.

exquisitely thrilling tone which all but obliterates the 'here and now' of the stage-picture in favour of a visionary picture of 'there and then'. It also (dependent on a conversion of the past 'might have been' into a future 'might be') points to the right true end of *Twelfth Night*.

During the life of the Voluntary, stage-movement is suspended, and it is with almost a jolt that the 'here and now' is resumed with

> *Vio:* Sir, shall I to this Lady?
> *Du:* I that's the Theame,
> To her in haste: give her this Jewell; say
> My love can give no place, bide no denay,

and the stage-picture once more becomes co-respondent with the verse. Nevertheless, though we (and the two characters) emerge from the Inset, it will continue to reverberate in the memory because, despite its seeming insulation from the dialogue forwarding the plot, it is the arcanum of the play where its essential 'meaning' is secreted.

But Cesario's Voluntary is not the only Inset in *Twelfth Night*, II. iv. It is balanced, earlier in the same scene, by Feste's Song, "Come away, come away, death". This tells of how another lover pined away to death because his passion was unreturned. This we shall consider in the next chapter. Meanwhile we turn to another, and a much earlier, example of the Voluntary.

2. DEATH BY DROWNING

The Voluntary in *Twelfth Night* is mature art. It could be by-passed entire—that is, cut in performance—without the loss of any essential link in the plot-chain. Yet it does make connection with that plot. In this way, the remote fictitious sister is a deputy for the speaker, Viola, and the man she loved is a deputy for Orsino. In the final act Viola and Cesario become identified with these projections.

In a much earlier play, though it is difficult to date, the connection between a Voluntary Inset and its environment is more difficult to perceive, still less establish. In his dream in *Richard III* (I. iv.), Clarence dreams that he was drowned.

Soon after he has narrated this dream, he is stabbed by one of
the murderers who then addresses the corpse:

> Ile drowne you in the Malmesey-But within.

Clarence dreams that he is drowned because he is knocked
overboard through a sudden lurch of his "Brother Glouster"
with whom he was promenading a ship's deck. Murdered,
through the cunning of Gloucester, Clarence's body is then
soused, in the butt of Malmsey dear to folk-memory and
mentioned in all of Shakespeare's sources, both certain and
merely possible. It might be thought that the connection
between Inset and play, on the basis of Clarence's dream of
being drowned and the total immersion of his body in wine
after death, is a weak connection. But "Brother Glouster" was
the agent of both dream death and actual death. Before
Clarence is killed, the First Murderer explains who had sent
them and on whose warrant they act. This undeceives the
victim as to the "kindness" of his brother. There is a
'Gloucester' link as well as a 'drowning' link connecting the
death with the dream of death which it so quickly follows.
The dream was prophetic.

Nor is the connection between Inset and *Richard III* localized
or limited to I. iv. 'Drowned off' in a fashion, after his dream
of being drowned, in the First Act, Clarence re-appears in the
Fifth Act as a Ghost in someone else's dream—his brother's,
the murderer's. A succession of his victims' Ghosts disturbs
Richard III's sleep in his tent before the battle of Bosworth
Field. When it comes to the turn of Clarence's Ghost it charges
Richard with his murder by drowning:

> I that was wash'd to death with Fulsome Wine:
> Poore Clarence by thy guile betray'd to death.

Clarence, in death, is angry with his brother not merely, one
feels, because his brother had him killed but because of the
way he had him killed—disgustingly "wash'd to death with
Fulsome Wine". It is as though he had been tumbled into the
butt while still breathing, and that the resentment is directed
less against the stabbing than against the subsequent ignominy
of being soused in wine. "Fulsome Wine"! The treatment of his
body was shameful or ludicrous, perhaps shameful because
undignified. It smarts the Ghost's memory and it may be that

Shakespeare has been persuaded by folk-memory of the manner of death of the 'good Duke of Clarence' to make this the gravamen of the Ghost's grievance in insisting that an obviously still living Clarence is dragged to the butt. Shakespeare's main source, Hall, had reported "The fame went that he [Richard] had the same night a dreadful & terrible dreame for it seemed to hym beynge a slepe that he saw diverse images lyke terrible divelles which pulled and haled him". Since there is no source authority for Clarence's dream in I. iv., this passage may have so impressed Shakespeare that he gave Clarence "a dreadful & terrible dreame" during his last night too. But Richard is to suffer as Clarence had suffered and Clarence is to haunt Richard's dream as Richard had haunted Clarence's dream. True, Clarence's dream is narrated while Richard's is shown. By choosing to show Richard's dream, Shakespeare projects the substance of the dream as ghost figures on the stage. Thereby Shakespeare anticipated both Posthumus' dream in *Cymbeline* and modern theatrical techniques. However that may be, the Ghost's appearance in Richard's dream in V. iii. connects this scene with Richard's appearance in Clarence's dream in I. iv. In I. iv. Clarence describes the dream he had suffered, a dream in which he had been knocked overboard by his "Brother Glouster" and so drowned. The relation between this Inset and its play is not confined to the connection between the Inset and the scene wherein it occurs.

Between the stage picture, which I. iv. presents, of a cell or dungeon in the Tower of London, and the Inset picture presented to the imagination of the audience, there is a striking contrast*. The theatre-audience is asked simultaneously to see (i) a physical picture composed of a prisoner and his keeper†

* "*Scene* The Tower" is the work of editors from Rowe onwards. Neither the Folio nor the Quartos prescribe 'the scene', but it is unnecessary that they should since the text (I. i.) explicitly declares that Clarence has been sent to prison in the Tower.

† Fi has 'Keeper', Qq 1–6 have 'Brokenbury' (*sic*) who is 'Lieutenant of the Tower'. The Folio is certainly correct in requiring the Lieutenant (Brackenbury) to relieve his underling when the prisoner has fallen asleep. There is a distinction of social tone and intellect. The speaker of "Sorrow breakes Seasons, and reposing houres" is officer-class. It seems that the confusion came about because in theatre practice the parts of 'keeper' and 'lieutenant of the Tower' were doubled.

in the oppressive frame of a dungeon; one man, unkempt and miserable, seated on a bench, and the other standing over him and equipped with that standard identifying hand-property, a bunch of keys, to 'see' (ii), in the imagination, a picture assembled by details, as vividly remembered and recounted by the prisoner, of a dream, a picture in which the dreamer was enfranchised from prison, was the observer of the substance of his dream and yet also a suffering participant. In his dream the dreamer enjoyed, in the legal sense of 'to be possessed off', enormous liberty of space (the English Channel and all the bottom-ooze below the Channel), and of movement (the ship was moving towards France but the dreamer could walk about on deck and promenaded by choice "Upon the giddy footing of the Hatches" until lurched overboard). There is thus a contrast between the physical picture of static confinement in a narrow cell and an imaginative picture of boundless air and sea. Yet Clarence, waking to the actuality of prison, was rather relieved than otherwise,

> I (trembling) wak'd, and for a season after,
> Could not beleeve, but that I was in Hell,
> Such terrible Impression made my Dreame.

Sidney, in a famous sonnet, had addressed Sleep as "the certain knot of peace", as "the balm of woe" and as "the *prisoner's release*", and Shakespeare was later to claim of Sleep that it knit up "the ravel'd Sleeve of Care" and was the "Balme of hurt Mindes", and might have agreed with Sidney in believing that it was "th' indifferent judge between the high and low". Anyone with humane feelings ought not merely to believe, but to hope, that *all* people are equally at peace while asleep, that prisoners are then as free as judges or gaolers. Yet here is a prisoner who in sleep was freed of his dungeon walls only to suffer an experience more harrowing than the experience of being a prisoner. Only in a state of dreamless sleep all men are equal and are all equally free, whether equal and free or not when they awake. But dreams are widely recognized by Shakespeare, and 'bad' (as we call them) dreams, and the fear of them, have their place outside *Richard III*—in *Romeo and Juliet*, *Macbeth* and *Cymbeline* for example, and the dread of them gives Hamlet pause.

Clarence then, seen sitting on a dungeon bench* with his gaoler standing beside him, is asked to explain why he looks "so heavily". Clarence replies that he has "past a miserable night" and that he

> would not spend another such a night
> Though 'twere to buy a world of happy daies.

The contrast is between the actual stage-picture of a miserable imprisonment and an Inset—or imagined—picture of a yet more miserable liberty; between an awake present and a sleeping past which is presently revived in the telling.

To the Keeper's "What was your dream my Lord, I pray you tel me", Clarence replies:

> Me thoughts that I had broken from the Tower,
> And was embark'd to crosse to Burgundy,
> And in my company my Brother Glouster,
> Who from my Cabin tempted me to walke,
> Upon the Hatches: There we look'd toward England,
> And cited up a thousand heavy times,
> During the warres of Yorke and Lancaster
> That had befalne us. As we pac'd along
> Upon the giddy footing of the Hatches,
> Me thought that Glouster stumbled, and in falling
> Strooke me (that thought to stay him) over-boord,
> Into the tumbling billowes of the maine.
> O Lord, me thought what paine it was to drowne,
> What dreadfull noise of water in mine eares,
> What sights of ugly death within mine eyes.
> Me thoughts, I saw a thousand fearfull wrackes:
> A thousand men that Fishes gnaw'd upon:
> Wedges of Gold, great Anchors, heapes of Pearle,
> Inestimable Stones, unvalewed Jewels,
> All scattred in the bottome of the Sea,
> Some lay in dead-mens Sculles, and in the holes
> Where eyes did once inhabit, there were crept
> (As 'twere in scorne of eyes) reflecting Gemmes,
> That woo'd the slimy bottome of the deepe,
> And mock'd the dead bones that lay scattred by.

* After reciting his dream, Clarence asks "Keeper, I prythee sit by me a-while, . . . I faine would sleepe". Not only is Clarence exhausted at the beginning of I. iv. but the verse here is of a kind that could not be naturally delivered standing.

The verse moves with great rapidity. This is appropriate since, although the speaker is utterly fatigued after the harrowing experience, that experience is still so pressing that he recounts it with fevered agitation, rush and urgency. What is remarkable is that such a vividly pictorial effect (pictorial in the sense that a painter might seize on the lines as a subject with the title 'Clarence's dream', believing that the poet prescribed every detail for his composition) is achieved with such a profusion of plurals and a series of large emotional pointers to a considerable, but vaguely known or uncounted, number. The picture does not come to focus on *a* skull, with reflecting and wooing jewels in its eye-sockets, though a painter might like to place one such skull in the centre of his design. If a listener, or reader, nevertheless has a mental picture composed of a single skull (with its artificial eyes), of a single wedge of gold, of a single great anchor and of one heap of pearl, and so on, as I suspect he does, then this is an interesting case of grammatical inflexions contradicting their formal signification. "Many thousands rendered homeless by Yang-Si flood" proclaim newspaper headlines, but the 'many thousands' is purely notional and the reader pictures either one homeless Chinaman or none and, if one, then the notional 'many thousands' is translated into a singular representative image.

Such an immediate translation from notional plurality into pictured singularity must be assumed to explain the pictorial vividness of the Inset, though some of Clarence's 'thousands' may be given the same sort of trust that we allow to the excited schoolgirl's use of 'millions'. Thus "upon the Hatches", Clarence "cited up a *thousand* heavy times", he thought he saw "a thousand fearfull wrackes" and "a thousand men that Fishes gnaw'd upon"—indeed the six Quartos agree that it was "Ten thousand" men that he saw "gnaw'd". Let the "thousand" or "ten thousand" stand for the notional 'ever so many', but the shipwreck must be singular, and the man being eaten by fishes must be singular to be imaged at all, but imaged with the notional reservation that wreck or man must be multiplied many times—must then be a repeating image.

The exaggerative plurality—the exaggeration true to pictorial dreams as well as to their febrile telling—in the "thousand" or "ten thousand" then passes to simple inflexional plurals, "wedges", "Anchors", "heapes of Pearle", "Stones", "Jewels", "Sculles", "holes", "Gemmes", "bones". Now the fact is that Shakespeare and Clarence are having it both ways: the notional plural is translated in each case into an imaged or imagined singular which is then notionally multiplied with reference to the reduplicative power of figures in dreams. A surrealist painter could have 'done' a painting of 'Clarence's dream' as easily as a nineteenth-century painter could have 'executed' an illustration of 'Clarence's dream' in an edition of Shakespeare. The 'dream' Inset of Clarence is brilliant writing and is vivid because the grammatical inflexions which normally produce cloudiness or a diffusion of pictorial impression are here used to double advantage. The effect is fortified by the haste with which the lines are uttered. Neither the stage-auditor (the Keeper) nor the theatre-audience are given time to image more than a representative example of each species— a wedge of gold, an anchor, a dead man's skull—and this it is which produces in both audiences' minds a firmly composed picture which can superimpose itself upon the actual spectacle of a prisoner and his guard in a cell.

The Inset picture does indeed narrow and focus upon the image of *a* skull, with glittering jewels in its sockets wooing "the slimy bottome of the deepe" and mocking the cross-bones and femurs scattered about it. But those "unvalewed Jewels" in the sockets are but part of an enumeration of riches, of "heapes of Pearle", of "Inestimable Stones", not counting the "Wedges of Gold". The skull, that emblem of death (multiplied), is associated in the dream with a vast display of littered wealth; the great anchors may be of rusted iron but all the other scatterings (except the "bones" which, like the "Sculles", are unnecessarily qualified by "dead" and are also "scattred") are massive demonstrations of gorgeous lost riches. Why? Dreams or night-mares are selective and do allow of sunken cargoes consisting only of treasure, though a diver stumbling along on the bed of the Channel would actually find much insoluble trash.

It is difficult not to associate the concluding focal image, singular but representative, of Clarence's dream—the skull with its glittering eyes which mock the piles of treasure—with renaissance and pre-renaissance iconography representing the Vanity of Riches or Riches and Death, and difficult not to associate it with the vision in Chaucer's tale of a pile of florins which *is* Death. And it is not altogether inconsequential that Clarence, who not only describes the substance of his dream but had participated in it, should soon be "wash'd to death with Fulsome Wine". Yet in the distress of the huge liberty of space that he had possessed in sleep, he had wanted to die:

> often did I strive
> To yeeld the Ghost: but still the envious Flood
> Stop'd in my soule, and would not let it forth
> To find the empty, vast, and wand'ring ayre.

No doubt, in a film version of *Richard III*, the director would be tempted to 'fade out' the 'setting' of the dream and present the dream itself, and probably he would be right if he yielded to temptation*. Less obviously related, even at depth, to the chain of plot of its play than is the Voluntary of *Twelfth Night*, it yet provides a medieval allegorical figure of Mortality and the Vanity of Riches, combined with suggestions of brilliance, waste and violence, that is an aptly summarizing figure for *Richard III*.

Clarence's dream is "lengthen'd after life". He is ferried over Styx by Charon to pass into the torments of a Classical hell. But the motive has now changed, and with it the tone, pitch and speed of the verse. The earlier phase of the dream had been a Voluntary, but when Clarence re-calls what the shade of Warwick cried out to him in Hell, and what the "Shadow like an Angell, with bright hayre/Dabbel'd in blood", it is plain that the Inset has become Expository and Plot-required. The theatre-audience is being informed that *Richard III* continues the matter of the contention between the Houses of York and Lancaster. It is given a revisionary course in the history of that matter and is reminded of Clarence's career in the scheme of the tetralogy.

3. THE DEAD WIFE

Our last example of a Voluntary Inset consists of seven-and-a-half lines.

* There was a film version of *Richard III*—and I was taken to see it. But I cannot remember how this Inset was treated.

In *The Winter's Tale*, IV. iv., the Shepherd scolds Perdita for not welcoming his guests arriving for the pastoral feast with enough show of cheerfulness. Florizel, just before, had entreated her not to look so downcast. "Be merry (Gentle)/Strangle such thoughts as these . . . . Lift up your countenance", and

> See, your Guests approach,
> Addresse your selfe to entertaine them sprightly.

Her foster-father now weighs in, following that cruel tendency in families whereby criticism advanced is supported and seconded by other members present. The Shepherd, and this too is a common family practice and a cruel one since the object of attack can hardly defend him- or herself without 'insulting' the memory of someone he or she scarcely knew, but who is idealized by a surviving contemporary through affection or loyalty, *compares* the living child's performance unfavourably with the dead parent's performance in a similar situation. The Shepherd, *laudator temporis acti*, shamefully takes advantage of his age:

> Fy 'daughter) when my old wife liv'd: upon
> This day, she was both Pantler, Butler, Cooke,
> Both Dame and Servant: Welcom'd all: serv'd all,
> Would sing her song, and dance her turne: now heere
> At upper end o' th Table; now i'th middle:
> On his shoulder, and his: her face o'fire
> With labour, and the thing she tooke to quench it
> She would to each one sip.

Compared with the Shepherd's dead wife on the occasion of this feast, his 'daughter' lacks vitality and 'outgoing' friendliness. Comparing Perdita, he criticises,

> You are retyred,
> As if you were a feasted one: and not
> The Hostesse of the meeting.

He is afraid that his reputation for hospitality will suffer unless she bucks up, so "Pray you bid/These unknowne friends to's welcome . . . . Come, quench your blushes". Goaded in this manner, Perdita does bestir herself. But she never approaches in her behaviour the bouncing energy, the Breughelesque heartiness of the peasant wife of the Inset picture. Perdita is a born lady, though bred a peasant, and she draws much attention to herself precisely because she is delicate. She draws more real admiration than the Shepherd's mirthful "old wife" ever drew in her lifetime at these annual junketings. Indeed, we can hope, for the sake of the Shepherd's past peace of mind, that the dead woman's energy so vividly realized in the picture, was met only by a coarse and temporary jollification as she appeared or leaned now "On his shoulder, and his". Because of Perdita's youth (she is sixteen), and because she is—though no-one knows it—a lady, it is doubtful whether this year's feast, even if no uninvited royal guests had turned up *incognito*, would have been unrestrainedly jovial. The old Shepherd had better live on his memories: there will be no good-natured, abandoned, ale-swilling, raucous-laughtered, humorous and unadulterous bottom-pinching, simple-hearted sheep-shearing Festivals at his homestead again.

Perhaps that is to exaggerate. The picture delivered by the lines is one of an open-air feast with rustics seated on the long benches and a hostess—flushed with excitement, exertion and drink, and superlative in her robust and ruddy vigour—being in all places at one and the same time, and leaning over the shoulder of now this guest and now that guest to sip to his health. But any attempt to define the picture results in a weak paraphrase with elements left out. The picture is one of extraordinary charm as well as of immediate force. Yet the bold and active life of these seven-and-a-half lines is achieved with the help of only a single adjective "old"; the rest is all nouns, verbs denoting being and doing, and adverbs—"now heere", "now". It is the concentration of these nouns and verbs and the near-total absence of the adjective* that gives the picture its realistic force: that and the rhythms which enact in movements of sound the pictorial constituents.

As for the single adjective "old". In its context this 'soft' element actually becomes 'hard' through its connection with "when", "upon this day", "would sing", "(would) dance", and the understood auxiliary "would" modifying the rest of

---

* Cp. Enobarbus' Expository Inset in *Antony and Cleopatra* ("the Barge she sat in . . .") which is loaded with adjectives. But these create the soft and langourous effect intended.

the verbs to the end. '*When* my old wife lived, then she would do *this* and do *that* on this occasion' is indeed the containing statement of the whole Inset. Within such a frame, "old" is rendered 'hard' because it does not simply denote the opposite of 'young'. She was not old when she cavorted about "upon this day"; nor was this day just once in the past, it was an annual occasion. The cavortings happened year after year until the young wife grew old, and died. The Shepherd's picture may be a capture in memory of his wife on one such particular occasion; but more likely it is a median image, an image drawn from the memories of a long series of feasts "upon this day" in which a diversity of incidents find a stabilizing centre. In such a median image the wife would be neither young (too little confidence) nor old (not enough energy), and the "old" of the Inset becomes a 'hard' linguistic element because it is not descriptive of age alone. 'My old bike', the bicycle may not have been 'old' but it was possessed long ago. The word further denotes affection—affection that has grown with use and familiarity ("habitual love", Pope calls it) if with nothing else. The word, combined with the "when" and the "woulds" (the "woulds" diminish, as the speaker makes his dead wife more and more present in memory, but are still to be understood), ensures that although the Inset presents a Breughelesque picture of romp and jollity it is tinted by hues of roseate melancholy. The Shepherd is a *laudator temporis acti*. His dead wife was a 'paragon'. It has been pointed out to me—and it is worth repeating—that in being an erstwhile 'paragon' she is a version of the greater 'dead wife'—Hermione.

Unlike the two Voluntaries earlier considered in this chapter, the scene of the Inset picture is identical with the scene of its frame—the Shepherd is "a man of fourscore three" and has presumably dwelt all his life at the place where he remembers what went on "upon this day". The time of both pictures is the same too, but only in the sense that anniversaries occur on the same day. In reality, however, anniversaries do not fall on the same day: an anniversary commemorates difference as much—or more—than sameness. When an anniversary 'comes round' it marks the passing of a year or the completion of an entire revolution of Nature. In *The Winter's Tale*, IV. iv., the Shepherd could be expected to remember "this day" (which was *not* 'this day') in years past—years (plural) for, as has been suggested, the image of the "old wife" is a median or fused image drawn or compounded from "this day" on *many* past occasions. The Inset could be cut from a performance without any injury at all to the theatre-audience's following of the "story", which the Inset interrupts, but much would be lost.

What would be lost would be a penetrative insight into the Shepherd's 'character'. The seven-and-a-half lines disclose his 'humanity', and also something about his history, a long history in which these annual feasts ranked as capital experiences. Yes, but this 'humanity' here disclosed is common 'humanity'—all people old enough to have a past to remember tend to remember it on appropriate occasions and no occasions are so appropriate as anniversaries and then the general temptation is to sentimentalize—that is, falsify—the past. It can hardly be claimed that the seven-and-a-half lines reveal the uniqueness of a 'character' since, on the contrary, they reveal the speaker to be 'common'—excepting that he does not sentimentalize. But the loss to the scene and the play, if the Inset were cut in performance, would not be confined to depriving the speaker of character 'depth'. The Shepherd is a representative 'voice' of a rural community; hence he is anonymous, designated in this Pastoral only by his pastoral following. He would be a person of no importance, since he is simply the Bohemian-Arcadian voice, but for his "luck" in finding "Faiery Gold" sixteen years earlier which makes him the agent of conservation in a tale of changing fortunes; but that "luck" (III. iii.) is going to turn 'unlucky' and he will find himself "undone" before *this* day is over.

Yet just because he is a mere voice of Bohemian-Arcadia it is important that he should sound its golden tradition (a myth?). Perdita is a novice at these affairs. This is her 'first time' as hostess. The memory commanded by "fourscore and three" is called on to spur her to take up and continue this tradition successfully. Within the terms of IV. iv. she fails disastrously (thanks to the unbidden guests she is goaded to welcome with more heartiness), so disastrously that the *laudator temporis acti* "desires" to "dye within this houre". Still, it is required not only that the Shepherd should have depth but that Bohemia-Arcadia should have depth; its oldest living inhabitant supplies

96

it when he remembers a golden past that was presided over by a kind of rural queen—his median image. Perdita is going to *be set* in perspective, poor girl, and appraised by remote ancestral example. She will fail because she is not born of that tradition. '*That* time a disguised princess presided and gentles intruded on simples' they will say years hence. She was not what she seemed though she is to be 'set' against a peasant wife.

The Voluntary Inset operates, beyond its own scene, on the whole play. Throughout *The Winter's Tale* the past has been set against the present (the past was exquisite); age against youth; experience against innocence. The Shepherd is going to contribute to this game, and so he does with results not pleasant to himself (for all the beauty and pathos of the past). The current is to change. The present is to be 'set against' the past; youth against age; innocence against experience. This is disturbing at first though eventually it produces what everyone accepts as good.

*   *   *

The Voluntary is the most interesting kind of Inset in Shakespeare because of its *seeming* irrelevance. In purely practical terms it suggested for the over-driven dramatist a variation of the fable that was richer than his sources provided.

VII. The Song Inset

Our concern, in this little book, is with the Shakespearean Inset; to note its appearance, to define its nature, to observe its kinds, to analyse its function. An Inset denotes a method whereby Shakespeare secures a variation of the dominant surface—from the point of view of the audience—of a play. The Inset marks a disturbance of the surface: a part of the play, more or less sharply demarked, presents a plane which contrasts with the plane of its surround. It is a matter of relief (as in '*bas*-relief'), and the variation in the surface secured by the Inset may be either by advance (or obtrusion) or by recession. Another mark of an Inset is that it produces a conflict, real or apparent, between what the audience sees and what it hears, a break in the fusion between Picture and Word.

We are accustomed to 'plane' to mean a level (e.g. 'so-or-so's conduct, or so-or-so's poetry is on an altogether higher plane than so-or-so's'), where the word is used of course metaphorically—for conduct or poetry cannot *really* be high or low—but, in fact, 'plane' also indicates degrees of relative distance and nearness as well as of height and depth. Certainly one can use 'plane', in its horizontal sense, of Shakespeare or any other poet, and say that some passages are in an 'elevated' style and some in a 'low' style (and many critics, for a hundred and fifty years, have precisely said this) and thereby communicate our sensitivity without harm, providing we do not deceive ourselves into believing that we are not employing a metaphor. But 'plane', in the sense of nearness or far-ness, has an equal or greater relevance in a discussion of Shakespeare—if not of

non-dramatic poets—for this reason: the reality called Shakespeare, the dramatic poet, only exists while one of the plays is
actually *being* performed, or—and this can be much better,
bearing in mind the limitation of producers, if not players—is
visualized as *being* performed while we are reading the text.
In either case, a series of moving stage-pictures, actual or
imagined, accompanies the language, and must be added to the
pictorial imagery bred by the verse. 'Plane', then, has relevance
because Shakespeare has real physical dimensions and one
of these dimensions is denoted by 'near' and 'far' in relation
to the distance between a part of the play and the audience
(or spectators).

One of the means whereby Shakespeare produces a variation
in the dominant surface of a play is the Song. This is un-
deniable; for a song marks a departure from the norm of
spoken blank verse as surely as a passage of speech would mark
a departure in an opera. Though Shakespeare's songs may vary
in merit, considered in isolation as lyrics, and though in their
contexts they may vary in purpose and function, they all have
this in common: the exchange of one vocal 'gear' for another.
Whether they were accompanied by musical instruments or
not, all the Songs—or fragments of Songs—involved a switch
from one kind of physical utterance to another. Singing is as
distinct from speaking as running is from walking. Speaking
is the Shakespearean norm (albeit that the delivery of blank
verse is a highly stylized mode of speaking), and when a Song
is introduced the disturbance in the linguistic norm is accompanied by, or brings about, a variation in the stage-picture.

The variation in linguistic surface started by a Song results in
a variation of pictorial perspective, usually by causing the
characters—who up to the entry of the Song may have occupied
the middle—or background—actually, or apparently, to
advance to the foreground. The Song reveals vistas behind the
characters. The characters are given a hinterland seeming to
recede, in some cases, without limit. From its position in the
hinterland, the Song casts on the foreground action while that
action is suspended—for, as with other Insets, the Songs tend
to render their stage-audience as captured and inert as the
paying audience in the body of the theatre—a light, or a comment, which could not be cast by other means.

To instance these remarks, consider the Song in *King Lear*,
III. ii.:

> He that has and a little-tyne wit,
> With heigh-ho, the Winde and the Raine,
> Must make content with his Fortunes fit,
> Though the Raine it raineth every day.

Here the light cast by the wise Fool on Lear's conduct, his
just and precise comment on Lear's folly, is achieved through a
Song, because the comment is sung and not spoken. It is not
only that the alternate rhyme (or near rhyme) and the free
octosyllabic quatrain form which differentiate the lines from
their blank verse context. These are certainly formal properties
of the Song and the contrast yields its effect. But the fact that the
words are sung and not spoken means, apart from any question
of the potentially immense emotive power of the human voice
when geared to song, that the words, or some of the syllables
of which they are constituted, receive the emphasis of protrac-
tion, and each line is emphasized by the longer pause that
occurs at the end of each line than occurs at the end of a blank
verse line. Further: that this particular Song is probably not of
Shakespeare's authorship, that it is instead a folk-song of
unknown authorship (or sounds like one), adds to the force of
its comment on the foreground action for Lear's folly is here
revealed and indicted, not by a licensed Fool, but by the
collective wisdom of all the dead generations. From the remote
background the ancestral past codifies its experience concerning
wind, weather, wisdom and fortune in a gnomic verse which
puts the behaviour of King Lear—in his here and now, in the
foreground of the stage-picture—to shame. The congregation
of all the dead (with the Fool as their instrument), who had
learned wisdom in their own time, is swelled by the addition
of the audience in the theatre. Unitedly, the dead and the
audience in the theatre perceive and pity Lear's folly. The dead
from the hinterland give the Fool his authority: he can here
sing what *they* say but which he would not speak in his own
person. He has indeed a "backing". And then, though the cap
fits only too uncomfortably exactly (though the pleasure of the
theatre-audience in a precise diagnosis co-exists with their
embarrassed pity), this Song has this power—here is not the

individual Fool speaking to the individual Lear but mankind singing to a man. The Song, in a Shakespeare play, is the general voice from a background generalizing on individuals in the foreground, and, if not always showing them up, showing where they stand*.

I. SAD LOVER

The Song that the Fool sings in *Twelfth Night*, II. iv. is also 'traditional'; it is an "old and Anticke song", such as

> The Spinsters and the Knitters in the Sun,
> And the free maides that weave their thred with bones
> Do use to chaunt.

Whether or no it is actually a folk-song, it is *passed* as such by Shakespeare. Orsino says that it has a haunting pathos

> More than light ayres, and recollected termes
> Of these most brisk and giddy-paced times,

and so it is more 'moving' than a modern Petrarchan lyric. Thus, though it is an 'I' song, and though it is entirely Petrarchan to the extent that a lover professes that he is dying or dead because a "faire cruell maide" will take no pity on him, yet the information that generations of "free maides", of spinners and knitters (so that we think of country-folk and not of courtiers) have sung what we are now going to hear for the first time (Orsino had heard it the previous night, but not in Cesario's—or our—company), will incline the theatre-audience to give it the respect due to a folk-song.

What the theatre-audience meanwhile is beholding is a court scene at a particular moment of time in the growth of the plot, in a timeless Illyria—timeless, but full of the historical period dream of Castiglione and his *Courtier*. Against this, the audience is told it is now going to hear an "old and Anticke" song, redolent of an English cottagey landscape and so introducing a far-stretching hinterland of ancestral folk experience to contrast with Orsino's amorous yearning, setting it in perspective.

* The refrain is actualized by the "Storm". According to the Stage-Direction it is raining and blowing. Thus the Inset Song is peculiarly adapted to its frame. A version of the same song ends *Twelfth Night* where it is less closely related to any particular phase of the action or to its frame.

Setting it in perspective! Generations of amorous yearners have suffered the pleasurable pains Orsino is suffering, sensations which the song indulges as much as it relieves. We prepare to measure the pains of Orsino, who does not die of his passion for a "faire cruell maide" against the pains of the 'I' of the song who says he does die. At the same time we also realize that there is no need for Orsino to die. His yearning is real enough but he will not die unless it is frustrated finally of an object*. Standing beside him is this 'Cesario' within whose masculine hose is (within the terms of this play) a vagina as willing to relieve the yearning as Olivia's is unwilling.

The Fool's Song in *Twelfth Night*, II. iv. then, like the Fool's Song in *King Lear*, sheds a light, or comments, on a character in the foreground action, though the depth from which it operates is less because the description of it as an ancient rural folk-song is hardly borne out by its text. Nevertheless the song does ring from out of the past to work on the here and now of the stage-picture, static during the song's rendering, laid before the spectators' eyes†.

The words of the lyric are those of a lover of the past declaring that he is "slaine"—he is sufficiently confident of his death to anticipate it—by a "faire cruell maide". He is slain because she will not assuage his desire for her body by allowing him to enter it. Despairing, the lover is concerned about his grave and his exequies. Because of the unkindness of his mistress, he does not want any of his friends to show their kindness or their affection by placing floral tributes on his coffin. This is childish or savours of sentimental self-regard. For why should the lover reject the rest of mankind because one woman is indifferent to his manic obsession with her body? Or perhaps this question is less commonsense than priggish. It could be retorted that

---

* We repeat: the yearning is real enough. Now this yearning, which is akin to the *angst* of loneliness, directed either at no particular object or at a mistaken and unresponsive object, deserves as much respect as a yearning which is shared by an object but which is prevented, or delayed, of fulfilment.

† For Feste is not singing his own story. It is firmly put in the past. The present "I am slaine by a faire cruell maide", etc. is framed by an understood perfect: 'Once there was a lover who complained as follows . . .'. The Song is enclosed by understood inverted commas, and is no more contemporary with the singer than is direct speech in a historical novel.

Feste's song precisely exemplifies the nature of frustrated amorous passion—that it is, depending on the intensity in which they are suffered, like other passions: ready, that is, to sacrifice all—everyone and everything—to possess its object and, despairing of possession, to reject all. Accepting this to be true (in which case it distinguishes the lover of a 'goddess' from the lover of God in whom all things are contained), it scarcely excuses this lover's egotism

> Not a friend, not a friend greet
> My poore corpse, where my bones shall be throwne.

All corpses are 'poore'. It is such an utterly evident truth that all corpses are 'poore', that to claim distinction for one's own carcass as noticeably poor is astoundingly arrogant or sentimental, or both. Sometimes a body is 'reverently interred'. Gently laid, or not, it is all one to the dead bones. This lover is pleased to fancy that his relics will be 'throwne', and then gives directions for his grave:

> A thousand thousand sighs to save, lay me o where
> Sad true lover never find my grave, to weep there.

This lover desires his obscurity to be so obscure that it is famous for its obscurity. "Sad" could mean 'serious' or it could mean 'grieving'. But it is more likely here to mean 'sad' in the modern sense. He here begs presumably for an unmarked grave lest a future lover, in the same woe-begone state as himself, should learn from an epitaph the cause of his death and sigh a million times in sympathy with a predecessor who had suffered the refusal of a "faire cruell maide". Well, it is probably true that sexual desire, if disappointed, can turn to a desire for death and that one can honey over the substituted object.

We have not been unjust to the meaning of the words of the Song which "relieves" Orsino's "passion much". At the outset we were told, by Orsino, that its text was not courtly-Petrarchan but rural-traditional but, by the last line, we might conclude that the Song is (i) less robust in its attitude towards death than a folk-song and is (ii) too pure-minded or clean for a folk-song. Contrast the *Unquiet Grave* or some of the songs of mad Ophelia when they touch on death and "country matters".

The Song is not as Orsino had described it, but it nonetheless puts Orsino in perspective and so fulfills its function.

Besides, having charged the Song in the manner of a moralist critic, it is only just to acknowledge three things.

The first is that most love songs—like most hymns—would be intolerably sentimental if they were said and not sung; very few could withstand 'critical scrutiny'. Abstracted from the melodies, which are less their accompaniment than environment, they disgust any mind which respects proportion. But couched in, wrapped around with, their music, sentiments and statements which would properly arouse ridicule or nausea, if they were spoken or read in dissociation or ignorance of the musical air which they inhabit, can command the most profound emotional, if not rational, assent. The British National Anthem, almost any other well-known National Anthem, "Rule Britannia", "Land of Hope and Glory", "Let auld acquaintance", etc., are evidence of this, and show that the generalization applies not to straight love songs and straight hymns but also to covert love songs and covert hymns. Things can be sung which cannot be said, providing a certain mood—which mood is conditioned by the company, or by the occasion, or by the alcohol, or by the hour of the day, or by a combination of all or any of these—is there.

The second thing to acknowledge in extenuation of the charges against Feste's song is that it only gradually reveals itself as other than Orsino had purported it to be, and as other than the theatre-, if not the stage-, audience had been prepared to accept. This is besides the fact that the music mitigates the mawkishness to the Song's end.

The third thing to acknowledge is that the whole strategy of the scene—considered both as Word *and* Picture—and that the whole conduct of the Inset, whereby the premises vouched on behalf of the Song are increasingly belied by the words, is deliberate on Shakespeare's part. That the stage-audience, with the exception of Orsino, should combine with the theatre-audience in concluding that the lover of the Song is mawkish and posturing is so probable as to be almost certain. The Inset of Feste's Song in II. iv. throws its light or comment, if not on the foreground action as a whole, then on one figure—Orsino. But, if on Orsino, then on the whole of the foreground action.

What then is the connection between the two Insets in II. iv.; between Feste's song, delivered for the benefit of Orsino, who takes it in one way, and for the members of the rest of both audiences, who take it in another way, and the Inset, which is a falsification, delivered by Cesario-Viola for the benefit of Orsino?*

There is, to start with, this connection: Feste's song of the Sentimental Lover so indulges, and in indulging, so stimulates Orsino's sentimental yearning for Olivia (in which pleasure and suffering are blended) that, after paying the singer, if not for his "paines" then his "pleasure", he tells Cesario to make another embassy to Olivia and this provokes the discussion on the nature of love which leads to the next Inset which is Viola's masked confession. Note that the passage between the two Insets is thoroughly 'here and now' and 'down-stage'. This between-passage indeed permits Feste to 'come out of it', to detach himself from that remoteness in which, as the performing soloist, he was the centre; it permits him to switch from the mode of singing to that of speech (and the switch is the more abrupt for it being prose speech) and to advance down-stage, transforming himself utterly from the sympathetic impersonator of the Sentimental Lover to his foreground character.

The other connection is more subtle. The two Insets both offer remote vistas or avenues receding from the immediately visible dominant plane of the Comedy confronting the theatre-audience. The formal connection of the two in depth will occur in the fifth Act, when the reality of the sex of Cesario is discovered. Until that solution the Song and Viola's Confession function as recessive columns set at right-angles to the façade; they are set in contrast—the fictional male lover's despair, and the fictional female lover's despair. Both fictional figures are eidola, deputies for the actual characters in the foreground. The eidola successively suspend all action in the foreground, freezing the picture while they are being formed. When the conduct of the plot is resumed, the eidola will, unseen though remembered, half-consciously, begin their flirtation, develop it, and, at the right moment, will inflict their desires and recognitions on the two characters who created them. The eidola will, at the end, occupy—or displace—their creators, become them and, in so doing, contradict their own earlier melancholy fates.

2. CONSIGN TO DUST

A Shakespeare play is ordinarily a compound of language and spectacle (though sometimes there are directions for non-linguistic sounds—drums, trumpets, thunder, etc.). But when a song is introduced there is a variation in the linguistic norm: instead of blank verse or occasional rhymed pentameter, rhymed strophes; instead of spoken words, sung syllables—with all the deflections from customary speech stresses (with consequent semantic and emotional transferences) this implies. Additionally, the sung syllables are accompanied by instrumental music, and the tunes can control and intensify the auditors' response. As to the spectacle, the song introduces a variation which it shares with other types of inset: stasis, or freezing.

In *Cymbeline*, IV. ii. a song is introduced which is not sung. Polidore (actually, in terms of the fable, Guiderius) and Cadwall (actually Arviragus) are to perform obsequies over Fidele (actually Imogen). Cadwall suggests they "use like note, and words" as they used at the burial of their supposed mother, Euriphile, except that since that event their voices "have got the mannish cracke". Polidore more frankly admits he "cannot sing" and will not try; instead he will

> word it with thee;
> For Notes of sorrow, out of tune, are worse
> Than Priests, and Phanes that lye.

So they resolve to "speake" or "say our song". Belarius goes off to fetch the headless body of Cloten, the supposedly dead Fidele is adjusted "with his head to th' East", and Shakespeare's greatest song, "Feare no more the heate o' th' Sun" is entoned by the two brothers over someone they believe to be a "Golden Lad" but which the theatre-audience (here there is no stage-audience) know to be a "Girle", a transvestite.

Unaccompanied by musical instruments, Polidore says the first stanza and Cadwall the second. The third and fourth are rendered antiphonally, each brother speaking single lines alternately. The final couplets

> All Lovers young, all Lovers must
> Consigne to thee and come to dust

and

> Quiet consumation have,
> And renowned be thy grave.

are rendered in unison.

Whether the Folio, as it has been argued, enjoins that the song be *spoken* because one or both of the young actors playing in the original or an early performance really discovered, when it came to the test, that their voices were breaking ("the mannish cracke"), or not, the rendering of the lyric in this way has powerful advantages. Not sung, the words—mostly massive, dirge-like, sonorous, long-vowelled—are still not said like blank verse. The rhyme, and semi-refrain, the metre ("Féare/ no móre/the héate/o' th' sún//Nór/the fúr/ious Wint/ers ráges"), all forbid this. So does the nature of the occasion, for it is a rite the brothers are celebrating. They are not 'inventing' what they say as they go along (and it is the supreme convention of Elizabethan drama that characters express themselves spontaneously in blank verse) because they have solemnized a death in this manner before now—when their supposed mother, Euriphile, died*. Because this is a rite, they 'entone' a rehearsed formulary, and 'entoning', if not singing, is still not spontaneous speaking, a distinction emphasized by the prepared distribution of the lines between the two mourners. Without any of the sweetening or any of the obfuscation of bare semantic force through a sentimental elongation of single vowel sounds at the dictation of an "ayre", this poem has all the ceremony of a funereal chant. Formal at the outset, the formality is intensified when, with the third stanza, the line by line antiphony is initiated.

---

* There is a puzzle. The brothers "use like note [except that they entone not sing] and words/Save that Euriphile [their supposed mother] must be Fidele". But since the name 'Fidele' does not occur, did the name Euriphile occur during the previous performance? And then, while "Golden Lads, and Girles" has application to Fidele-(Imogen) since she is both lad and girl, what application had it to the matronly, and possibly aged, Euriphile?

The spectacle is as ceremonial as the language—'dead' Fidele-Imogen lies supine in the near- or middle-distance of the stage-picture, the brothers Polidore-Guiderius and Cadwall-Arviragus stand statuesque beside the corpse.

After

> Quiet consumation have,
> And renowned be thy grave.

Morgan-Belarius enters with the headless body of Cloten, and then mobility is restored to the picture, blank verse to the language, and the Inset is over.

What experience has the Inset transmitted? However tender, sweet-sad and nature-redemptive the scenes laid near Milford Haven in Pembrokeshire have hitherto been, it has been difficult to accept either Imogen's adventures or their setting as other than stray, tenuous in the narrative line, singular and so frontal. The formal language of the dirge, and the formal picture which accompanies it, gives depth and generality. Even though Fidele-Imogen is not dead in his/her 'death' he/she shares part of the 'all' who "consigne to thee [death, and the rule of Nature] and come to dust". Dead, he/she surrenders to a law whose gravity and universality had hitherto been kept out of range. The setting of the dirge will be altered by this: the song itself secures the depth-penetration but this will colour the whole series of 'Wild Wales' scenes. But the song's influence is not limited to endowing its surround with a mellow but sombre tone. The four stanzas consign Fidele-Imogen to the common death of the golden lads and girls but, in their progression, refer to the great themes and divisions of the drama. Thus the first stanza, said by Polidore-Guiderius, and beginning

> Feare no more the heate o' th' Sun,
> Nor the furious Winters rages,

states the theme of exposure to all weathers—of Nature, and of Nature as opposed to the Court (cp. *As You Like It*, *King Lear*)—which is the concern of the series of Wild Wales scenes. Morgan-Belarius, Euriphile, the two boys had chosen the harsh discipline of cave-dwelling, hunting and Nature (as, long before, the Exiled Duke of *As You Like It* had accepted "Winter and rough weather" and, having accepted, had preferred it to the

Court) in preference to a corrupt Court. The honest discomfort, or ferocity, of Nature is a counter to the dishonest ferocity of the Court. Very well, and Imogen, who has discovered the one, will discover the other as Fidele.

But the second stanza, said by Cadwall-Arviragus, and beginning

> Feare no more the frowne o' th' Great,
> Thou art past the Tirants stroake,

points to the harms and dangers risked in—in Shakespeare—that opposite remove to Nature, the Court. Political power, learning, even medicine (metropolitan, academic or urban things) are as frail as golden lads and girls.

The third stanza is antiphonal: the pair of brothers entone alternate lines, but what they say means that Fidele-Imogen is 'past' both, is beyond feeling either natural or human malice:

> P–G. Feare no more the Lightning flash.
> C–A. Nor th' all-dreaded Thunderstone.
> P–G. Feare not Slander, Censure rash . . .

yet, to the theatre-audience, Imogen is—as she seems to be—dead because of the human "Slander" and the Court "Censure". Nevertheless he/she is a "lover young" who must consigne to death and come to dust.

The final stanza, which is antiphonal:

> P–G. No Exorcisor harme thee,
> C–A. Nor no witch-craft charme thee.
> P–G. Ghost unlaid forbeare thee . . .

is a pretty, yet necessary, extension of the three preceding stanzas. Fidele is 'past' suffering from either Nature's harshness or the Court's malice, but she is still vulnerable to supernatural disturbance or injury. May he/she be "Quiet", the brothers together enjoin, and

> renowned be thy grave.

The Song Inset has pooled the issues and divisions of *Cymbeline*. It is the centre and microcosm of *Cymbeline*; but it only achieves this by a suspension of the give-and-take in the here-now of the drama by interposing a frozen group in a picture which relates to a meaning at depth, so distant in perspective that it is off-stage and yet undeniably framed.

3. OWL AND CUCKOO

The song at the end of *Love's Labour's Lost* is exquisite beyond all compare. Or nearly beyond compare, for in *As You Like It* Amiens has a fine song about early summer ("Under the greene wood tree") and yet finer about winter ("Blow, blow, thou winter winde"): but the separate members are—so to speak—combined, combined yet opposed in the two-fold song of *Love's Labour's Lost.*

The two songs in *As You Like It* are profoundly embedded in their contexts, the second especially—though that may be not an issue of Shakespeare's art but of general human psychology*. They are genuine Insets in that, though while these songs are being sung and the stage picture is still or the stage-auditors are motionless, the dominant themes of the play are being both absorbed and radiated. Can the same be said of the combined summer-winter song at the end of *Love's Labour's Lost*?

At first sight, or hearing, the song in *Love's Labour's Lost* might seem less of an 'embedded' entity, less reflective and re-distributive of the themes of its context, than a kind of coda in the manner of Feste's last song in *Twelfth Night*. It is tacked on and, it might be argued, it is detachable and, detached, the winter half, if not both halves, makes a beautiful self-sufficient number in an anthology of lyrics. The play could end, if not like "an old play", yet with the lines

> *Berowne:* Our woing doth not end like an old Play:
> Jacke hath not Gill: these Ladies courtesie
> Might wel have made our sport a Comedie.

and thereby more pointedly seem to consummate the play's title. But the Comedy does not end there. If it did it would be too abrupt, or too sour, a conclusion, like that of a problem comedy of the *Troilus* period; the *exeunt* of the King of Navarre and his men in one direction and the *exeunt* of the Princess of

---

* I.e. That the wintry and *grave* (the etymology of 'grave' points the tautology) affects more *profoundly* than the summery and light-hearted. This truth, if it is truth, will partially explain the superiority of *hiems* over *ver*—in art or popular favour or in both—in the song to be discussed.

France and her ladies in the opposite direction would be too sharp.

Too sharp, although there must be an eventual division, for the last words of the Braggart are

> You that way; we this way.

which, though variously interpreted as a dramatist's stage-direction by producers of the play in practice, really do point to a dividing of the ways not as between gentles and others—as is sometimes wrongly done—but as between the sexes. The men, whether courtiers or countrymen, and the women, whether ladies or bumpkins, leave the stage through opposite doors like the queue issuing from a touring coach bifurcating outside a so-called public 'toilet'*—opposite for love's crown is lost for a "twelvemonth and a day" and, in the case of the Braggart, for "three yeares". But to lose for a year and a day is not to lose for ever, nor does the postponement make for a sort of 'problem' comedy. Yet there is some need to realize what a year—that measure of human age—is. The song makes clear what a year, natural and calendar, is as does no other song: it is a temporal cycle and it includes a summer and a winter. Self-sufficient in whole or in half as an item in an anthology the song may be, but it has a relevance to the play it concludes. It illustrates the preceding dialogue on the period of time in which Navarre and his men must labour before love can be won.

Nor does the song end the play. When it is finished the Braggart speaks three lines:

> The Words of Mercurie,
> Are harsh after the songs of Apollo:
> You that way; we this way.

and thereby the song is built-in—becomes an Inset. Cancel that speech of the Braggart and more is lost than the final

---

* Vile word 'toilet', and post-war international, displacing the nearly as vile 'convenience' (which became rude) which succeeded to 'lavatory' (which became rude) which succeeded W.C. 'Gents' is bad, and so is 'Ladies'. Shakespeare's word is *jakes*, honouring the English inventor Sir John (Jack) Harrington, and Shakespeare's word is good, though perhaps modern American john is better. Lecturing on *The Rape of the Lock* one has to tell undergraduates not to titter at a deforming notion of Belinda at her toilet and that to be genteel is to offend against the great language.

stage-direction (if the stage-direction is obeyed there is created an exact pictorial equivalent of the language and of the intention of the play as a whole). The words themselves are sweet but poignant. Is speech itself harsh after song? Or are just the words "You that way; we this way" Mercury's instruction and that a harsh one? This cannot be determined, but if the speech is cut, the song, instead of being built in, becomes a mere appendage much like the dance following the last words of *Much Ado*.

The Braggart describes the song as a Dialogue "in praise of the Owle and the Cuckow" and says that "It should have followed in the end of our shew". Whatever application it might have had to the Shew of the Nine Worthies, what background does it provide, however late in the day, for the comedy into which it is built? The answer must be that it sets the affectations and self-deceiving aims of Navarre and his academy in perspective. The song *celebrates* the opposing seasons, summer and winter, comprising the year. Unlike the two lines

> Feare no more the heate o' th' Sun,
> Nor the furious Winters rages,

in *Cymbeline* (which in thirteen short words states the two seasons as in opposition yet both ferocious) this year—Nature's and human life's unit of count—is now accepted as charming. And why not? Since there is no avoidance of an opposition and a rhythm which is Nature's—though Navarre and his academy have attempted, or pretended to attempt, to contract out—it might as well be accepted as charming. No dead Fidele is to be at once mourned and consoled; rather what are dead are some youthful and vain pretensions. By the end of a "twelvemonth and a day" Navarre and his academy, who have been devoted to a false learning hostile to life, will have learned to accept nature or the year.

Both halves of the year in the song in *Love's Labour's Lost* are charming as both halves—presented in two lines—are harshly merciless in the song of *Cymbeline*. There is no simple opposition of the 'summer is all joy, winter is all misery' kind in the *Love's Labour's Lost* Inset because both seasons are accepted (as in *Cymbeline* both are rejected). In the "Dialogue that the two

Learned men have compiled", summer has its anxieties and winter its cheerful compensations; the "Cuckow" sounds its displeasing "word of feare" in summer and the "Owle" sounds its "merrie note" in winter. But both seasons are mainly cheerful.

Navarre and his fellow-students should grow up and meanwhile hear about life, not as lived within a grove of academe, which is an enclosed royal parkland, but outside—beyond the palings in the open countryside.

If the winter stanzas are more anthologized than the summer stanzas, and are more generally taken to heart, it is more because Dick, Tom and "greasie Jone" and Marrian are personalities than that schoolchildren are likely to enquire about the meaning of "Turtles tread" (*and* Rookes *and* Dawes) or to ask why "Cuckow" should be "Unpleasing to a married eare". The summer half is very beautiful but the *plurals*, "Shepheards", "Ploughmen", "Maidens", "married men", combined with other *plurals*, "Oaten strawes", "merrie Larkes", "summer smockes", let alone the three kinds of amorous birds, conduce to an effect both distancing and generalizing. Contrasted with this diffusion (which I believe to be subtle and purposeful art), the winter half presents particularizing close-ups and hence Dick, Tom, Jone and Marrian by name; and where, in the case of the parson, there is no name ("And coffing drownes the Parsons saw"), the grammatical number is still singular*. Of course "Tom beares Logges" but he bears them "into *the* hall"; of course "Milke comes frozen home" but it does so "in paile"; and of course "birds sit brooding" but they do so "in *the* snow"; and there are "roasted Crabs" "in *the* bowle"; and—finally—plural "Isicles" hang by the singular "wall": against this concentration of many into one the summer half is full of plurals, both subjective and complementary—"Dasies", "Violets", "Ladiesmockes", "Medowes". The line "And merrie Larkes are Ploughmens clockes" should, as a plural effect, be compared with "And Dick the Shepheard blowes his naile". Against the eighteen plural substantives of 'Summer' there are five in 'Winter'.

* In a parish he would be the—because the only—parson; and to give him a name, even if it were metrically possible and socially proper, would be to de-particularize.

Whether in Shakespeare or out of Shakespeare, and whether in his time or ours, the English summer is more tolerable than the English winter is not the question. The point is that, here in the Dialogue, Winter is a close-up, homely, personal, vivid and (in a metaphorical sense) warming, while Summer is delightful and refreshing but distant and so relatively vague. Add: the cuckoo is disturbing and the owl is comforting and cosy.

What has all this to do with the play, *Love's Labour's Lost*; to which at the last gasp it supplies an Inset? This much: the King of Navarre, and his fellow-dilettantes, are to gravely discover, for the space of "twelvemonths and a day", the truths of nature. The Princess of France tells Navarre to rough it for that space of time in "some forlorne and naked Hermitage". There no doubt the winter will be grimmer—and longer—than the summer, but that at the end of this "annuall reckoning"

> If this austere insociable life,
> Change not your offer made in heate of blood:
> If frosts, and fasts, hard lodging, and thin weeds
> Nip not the gaudie blossomes of your Love,

she will be his. In the light of this penance, was it kind of the Nine Worthies to sing of the social jolliness of winter? But the song reveals the order of nature and an order of human living which are real, from which Navarre and his fellow-students have withdrawn themselves but to which they may return.

The song, with the stage-auditors as captive as the theatre-audience, spreads out, both at the time it is being sung in a performance and after the performance is over, to temper the whole play. The exquisite posturings of Navarre and his academicians, which nevertheless have a kind of grace and a beautiful pathos, are placed in perspective. The follies of a season are set in foreground relief against the recurring pattern of the year.

* * *

The Song Inset in Shakespeare can discover perspectives of various depths. The work of each song must be considered in its context. It is not so much a question of whether this or that song is pretty or touching or, occasionally, even majestic,

when it is sung or read in isolation, or even whether Shakespeare was the author or had incorporated a folk-song, but
rather a question of its function. The question should be:
What does this song do to its play in return for interrupting its
action? To that part of the play preceding the interruption as
well as to that part which follows?

VIII. The Insets of Hamlet

Macbeth has an action animated by prophecy and geared to ambition; the action ordains that the play is future-directed. In *Othello* the protagonist is given to reminiscence; he remembers his old campaigns while wooing Desdemona; he remembers the manufacture of a handkerchief; he remembers what he once did in Aleppo. These pockets of memory apart, this play lives almost throughout from moment to moment in its own present—looking neither before nor after: for Othello's anguish is present anguish and nothing lightens it until he fastens his thoughts and purposes on "a capeable, and wide Revenge"—that is, until he can work on something to be concluded in the future. In *King Lear*, as one would expect, there are backward glances (e.g. when Lear in I. iv. painfully replies "No more of that, I have noted it well" to a Knight's reminder that the Fool had "much pined away" since Cordelia's going into France) and there are forward glances as each intention is framed with a "I will . . . " or a "I shall . . . " this or that, thus moving the present "is-ness" forward so that it becomes a "was". In *Antony and Cleopatra* there is recollection (by Antony of his former soldierly greatness, by Antony in his nostalgia for Egypt while in Rome, by Enobarbus of a lovers' first meeting) and anticipation (Antony, late in the play, believes "There's hope in't yet", and that he will beat the Romans to their beds). In these great Shakespearean plays there is naturally some hind-reference and some fore-reference. In all there is naturally some swing in time back and forth, naturally some remembrance or remorse, some desire or hope; yet all, of course, live and grow in their *now*—even *Macbeth* which is avid for the future and where Lady Macbeth can say "I feele now/The future in the instant".

Against these plays *Hamlet* stands in a peculiar situation. For this reason: Hamlet is bidden by his father's ghost "Remember me" and this injunction to remember is to be the spur to "Revenge his foule and most unnaturall Murther". Remember and Revenge. Hamlet is set between them: the one is an act of mind directed to the past, the other is energy directed towards the future. The future is to be darkened by the past. Meanwhile the present, the *now*, is to be stretched, perplexed, nearly annihilated between the strain exerted—between the past ("Remember") and the future ("Revenge"). "Looking before and after", Hamlet, and indeed *Hamlet*, is subjected to tension. Thus it is not surprising that this play is compact of Insets, salient or recessive, and that these Insets connect with each other—salient with salient, recessive with recessive—either in front of, or in the background of, the dominant surface plane presented to listeners *and* spectators. For the 'audience' also *watch*, they are as much ringside fans at a wrestling match as they are Promenade Concert goers*.

Behind Hamlet in time is a murder which he is bound by oath to revenge in the future. So the whole of the presented action (up to the killing of Claudius near the end of Act V) is perplexed or shadowed by a completed deed at a definite point in the past which demands a retributive deed at an indefinite point in the future. Held taut between these two points in time, the play consequently refers to that past murder and that future: it provides, therefore, Insets of a retrospective there and then and a prospective there and then in the midst of the here and now. In 'The Murder of Gonzago' the retrospective and the prospective would seem to unite. 'Would seem to' unite rather than really unite: for the 'Murder', "writ in choice Italian", whether regarded as Dumb Show or as a text, or as both, was—unless the Ghost had particularized further in private—a reflection of Hamlet's reflection on the past and only an approximate pointer to the consequence pitched in the future.

* Yes, but, it will be objected, at a wrestling match the result might go either way while the determination of Beethoven's Fifth Symphony in C Minor is well known from the score. But (again) in 1603 the score of *Hamlet* was as unfamiliar, or as unknown, as the spectacle, and in 1964 the spectacle, not the score, is much at the disposal of the producer.

But in *Hamlet* there are pasts other than Hamlet's and ghosts other than Hamlet's father's. Behind the scene laid in Elsinore, visible to the spectators, is Norway; also behind the visible scene is France, and the seas between Denmark and England, and—in Q2—a "little patch" or "plot" of Poland. These concerns are not 'off-stage' or 'in the wings' but behind what is physically presented to the audience; in turn each will advance and invade the physically visible. Meanwhile, how the bed-ridden old King of Norway deals with his keen-spirited nephew; how Laertes is sowing wild oats in France; how the pirates were tackled during a skirmish between two ships in the North Sea; how young Fortinbras is likely to fight in Poland after his passage across Denmark—all these 'hows' are delivered to the ears of the audience while, as spectators, their eyes are occupied with the 'here and now' of the Royal Court of Denmark.

Wilhelm, very much a persona for Goethe himself, in the now little-read novel *Wilhelm Meister*, intended to take a production of *Hamlet* on tour. As the producer, Wilhelm considered the diversity of non-Danish interests too liable to confuse the audiences in those German towns where his wandering actors are to mount their show and to whom *Hamlet* will be new. This dispersion was a danger. So he resolved to fuse these interests into a single "background action"—a Norwegian affair—centring about Fortinbras. Hence Laertes travels to Norway and not to France; hence Hamlet is to be shipped to Norway, whose king has strong reasons for obeying Claudius' request, and not to England. Through this amalgamation, Wilhelm believes, there would be this gain: that Norway, much mentioned in the early scenes, subject of old dispute between the dead Hamlet and the dead Fortinbras, will increasingly press forwards, so that when, at the conclusion of the play, young Fortinbras entered the corpse-littered palace at Elsinore to claim the crown of Denmark, there would visibly emerge to the fore the embodiment of the mounting background theme. If modern producers reject Wilhelm Meister's plan for a concentration of non-Danish interests, they should at least recognize that Goethe perceived the truth that in Shakespeare —and Shakespeare exists while a play is being performed, or is envisaged as being performed—there are vertical planes of nearness and distance between the play and the audience; that he recognized that behind the pictorial composition that a play presents at any one moment to an audience there can exist background pictures not less real for not being physically composed on the stage. In *Hamlet* especially, an audience is aware not only of the murder, anterior in time to the presented action but still shadowing that action, but also of simultaneous activities remote from the Danish Court in space yet pressing on the visible scene. Laertes in France, Fortinbras in Norway or Poland, Hamlet on the high seas for England—what they are doing while the audience is beholding an interior of Elsinore Castle will affect that interior, but so also does the defeat of old Fortinbras at the hands of old Hamlet x years ago.

Hamlet is also crowded with Insets because it is full of espionage and eavesdropping. Reynaldo spies on Laertes and Polonius eavesdrops on Hamlet; Hamlet eavesdrops on the Gravediggers and the Gravediggers spy out Yorick. The theatre-audience will not watch 'The Murder of Gonzago' merely through the stage-auditor, Claudius. Rather, they will watch it through Hamlet as he watches Claudius as Claudius watches 'The Murder of Gonzago'. When Ophelia is loosed before Hamlet, the encounter is overwatched and overheard by Polonius and Claudius, and the theatre-audience is invited to consider the nature of the past and present relationship between Hamlet and Ophelia, its history, not only directly but mediately —through the judgment of the spies and eavesdroppers, though these differ between themselves as to the nature of Hamlet's illness. Hamlet keeps his eye on Claudius; Rosencrantz and Guildenstein watch Hamlet so as to report back to Claudius; Polonius dispatches Reynaldo to Paris to trail Laertes. And so on. All is oblique.

Hamlet is Henry Jamesian in its obliquity. The theatre-audience can certainly see what the producer arranges to have laid out before their eyes on the stage. And let us suppose the producer lays out what the author intended to have laid out— still there is an obliquity. In other Shakespeare plays the audience can take on trust, and in justified innocence, what is shown on the stage—even after taking into full account some critics' doctrine of 'Appearance and Reality'. Good men and villains elsewhere declare themselves to the audience if not to fellow characters. In the case of *Hamlet* this is not so, and the difference is only partially explained by saying that *Hamlet* is a dramatized novel of crime and detection. For though there had been a murder, Hamlet is no detective who has to discover the guilty conscience behind the innocent countenance. He is no detective because he is informed by a supernatural agent, at the outset, both as to the name of the guilty man and his motive. There is no mystery there. Rather, the theatre-audience have to regard what they see before them on the stage with suspicion because they are invited, by one after another character, to see not for themselves but through the character's eyes. In this process a series of vistas or Insets are opened up which clash with the visible scene—avenues or columns of recession involving times and places other than the time and place before the audience. The imaginative pictures provided by these Insets can be more compelling than the physically visible picture. At the least they can modify that picture so that its lines, its whole composition, becomes questionable. These Insets include examples of each kind that we have so far considered.

I. THE EXPOSITORY INSET

"Something's rotten in the State of Denmark"—this line, while it usually raises a laugh, is by and large accepted as a key; some moral corruption, resembling physical corruption, exists within the Danish Court. The audience is less aware of external menace. They are ready to accept the sentinels as performing normal rather than exceptional guard-duties "on a platform before the castle"*. Certainly there is an un-ease and a tensed-up vigilance but this is because the Ghost has twice appeared to the sentinels and they nervously expect a third visitation, and receive it. The Ghost is a "dreaded sight" and the audience, responding to the dread of the sentinels, are infected by it. Dread is a species of fear; and fear is one of the three primal instincts as psychologists and biologists tell us. Fear is even more fundamental than the instincts of love and aggression, for it is

---

* The stage-direction is Rowe's. Modern producers prefer to convey the sense of a battlemented platform at an elevation. But this follows from the practice of playing I. i. up-stage.

indisputable that an organism must preserve itself alive in time before—and until—it can reproduce itself and then protect its young.

However it might be as to primacy among the primary, it is a fact that *fear* is generic and that there are a number of species— fright, terror, alarm, etc.—of which dread is one. What distinguishes dread from—say—terror is that, whether or not it rests its apprehension on previous experience of danger or harm, it is anticipatory in nature. The sentinels, at the start of I. i., dread lest the Ghost *will* appear, or re-appear. If, and when, the Ghost *does* appear they will be frightened or terrified: until then they dread. For the purposes of poetry, whether dramatic or narrative, no species of emotion is so powerful as dread. It sucks the life-blood, as Coleridge says, through the person of the Ancient Mariner when he describes the spectral ship.

To support this, consider: when the dreaded thing is expected the characters may talk of the object of their dread or the poet may describe it, but in the object's presence the characters are either speechless with terror or they run away, or they defy the object because retreat is impossible or its penalty worse than facing up to it. Horatio hails the Ghost in I. i. and thereupon it stalks away in offended silence. Hamlet defies the Ghost in I. v. and then it beckons, urging him to follow it, which he does. Dread gives way to terror, or rather desperation, and terror to pity, when the Ghost reveals his identity in conversation. Brutus confesses dread ("Between the acting of a dreadful thing,/And the first motion, all the Interim is . . ."); Macbeth dreads before he acts. Brutus' dread and Macbeth's dread make for supremely powerful pieces in Shakespeare, but once Hamlet has accosted the Ghost there is no more dread. The audience indeed do not experience even terror again. The Ghost, when it re-appears without warning in III. iv., raises awe in Hamlet, and amazed concern in Gertrude who sees her son's eye "bending on vacancy"—for she beholds no Ghost—but the audience feel no terror since they have anticipated none. There is no dread after the early scenes; nor is there any dread there once Hamlet gets going in speech with his talkative father's ghost.

But in I. i. the power of the anticipatory emotion of dread— stimulated by a report of the Ghost's appearance on two earlier occasions, its likely reappearance, and sustained even after its third appearance (which brought terror) because its identity and purpose remains unknown—is so strong that it spreads like a stain to colour the following Inset about old Fortinbras, about young Fortinbras, about the *raison d'être* for the exceptional guard-duties, about this

> most observant Watch,
> That nightly toyles the subject of the Land.

It spreads like a stain to colour what might have been a dull recital of facts, a recital as dull as the exposition of the Salic Law in *Henry V*. The recital is tense and dreadful not because of its own intensity or dreadfulness but because of a kind of *sostenuto*. The dread, previously generated in a discussion about the Ghost, is still throbbing when the answer is given to the question "Why this same strict and most observant Watch?" Exceptional guard-duties are in force because of the threat of a Norwegian military invasion. The particulars of that menace, and its history, forms the subject of an Inset. But had Shakespeare chosen to reverse the order of exposition concerning (*a*) the Ghost question, and (*b*) the Norwegian question, we could not listen to legal arguments about a "Moity" of lands with hearts beating more quickly than normal—which we do, thanks to the emotion of dread aroused by expectation of the Ghost, which is stimulated by its appearance, and which then takes time to subside.

Nevertheless the sentinels sit down to be informed:

> Good now sit downe & tell me he that knowes
> Why this same strict and most observant Watch,
> So nightly toyles the subject of the Land.

and to that extent there is a relaxation of tension, some easing precisely signified by the mere act of sitting. Thus the change from the dramatic mode to the narrative is signified by a change in the attitudes of the figures forming the pictorial composition on the stage. And the vocal tone alters with "Tell me he that knowes". Marcellus asks

> . . . why such dayly Cast of Brazen Cannon
> And Forraigne Mart for Implements of warre:

Why such impresse of Ship-wrights, whose sore Taske
Do's not divide the Sunday from the weeke,
What might be toward, that this sweaty hast
Doth make the Night joynt-Labourer with the day . . .

Why? Why? (And why doesn't the Union of Shipwrights protest against a 72 hour week?) Marcellus' questions are going to prompt a narrative poem, deposited in a dramatic text, which is going to drive a column, or corridor, into the past, into history, and this column or corridor is aiming—or seeming to aim—at setting what we are going to see (the here-now of the Danish Court) in perspective; that is, to endow the otherwise flat picture of a Court-scene with the dignity of an unseen—but felt—ominous background. In the presentation of a here-now of the façade of a building, with no speculation provoked as to what might lie behind it, there is no hope, no interest, no awe, no possibility; the same is nearly true of a theatrical scene Marcellus, by his 'Why's', is certainly going to 'connect' the pulse-quickening dread of the Ghost with political history (the past) and with the "nightly toyles" of sentinels *and* with a seven-day working week. Even so, he—or rather Shakespeare—is counting on the diminishing, but not yet extinct, dread of the Ghost (neither its identity nor its motive is explained yet) to sustain and colour not only the otherwise prosaic questions but the still more prosaic replies. The speech of Marcellus is great poetry and is made so (not '*but* is made so') because of what preceded it. Yet if not 'great' when isolated, i.e. when it is heard in detachment from what precedes, it is at least sinewy. For proof of this, consider the shifts of tense and grammatical mood employed by Marcellus in his list of questions, the change —for example—between 'Do's' and 'might be', with a return to the Active Present 'Doth make' and concluding with a 'Who is't'. Certainly, the positioning of this introduction to the retrospective narrative marks a new wisdom—gained by the hardest way, by experience—in the subtle but necessary task of informing an audience of an anterior situation, of presenting an Expository Inset.

And so they sit—the four of them—in a huddled semi-circular group down-stage while the Narrator (Horatio) gives his stage-listeners and (through them) the theatre-audience a slice of history, a bit of 'then-there'. But the 'then-there' is linked to the 'here-now':

> Our last King,
> Whose Image even but now appear'd to us,
> Was (as you know) by Fortinbras of Norway, . . .
> Dar'd to the Combate. In which, our Valient Hamlet . . .
> Did slay this Fortinbras.

The last king is a dead king, a 'late' king, is a king who 'was', but here he 'is'—or, at least, he appeared 'even now'. The "Time" may be "out of joint" in this, but the effect of the placing of Shakespeare's Expository Inset after, and not just before, the third apparition of the Ghost (so that the "Valient Hamlet"—Hamlet I—who was, *is*), is to narrow the gap between the present and the past, between the 'here-now' and the 'there-then' of history.

Previously, in Shakespeare's career, we had learnt to be prepared to stifle yawns at some point in I. i., while the 'action' would seize up, the pictorial *assemblage* on the stage would become 'frozen', and a player would do some 'distancing'. On those occasions, a character—the stock example is Egeon—would recite to a frozen stage-audience a long narrative, intended not really for them at all (though the stage-listeners may have to feign expressions of astonishment) but for the theatre-audience. As a result the theatre-audience gained information necessary for their understanding of what was going on but—an accompanying result—the theatre-audience, having heard the action's pedigree, dismissed it. That is, the audience drew off what was necessary for their following of the mechanics of the plot and forgot the rest. Their danger in consigning the rest to oblivion was that the series of pictures they were about to see on the stage would have no colouring background; or, if something remained, it would be arbitrary and selective, relating to cause-and-effect elements only. It would be separated from the 'here-now' by a conventional and factitious temporal dimension, and the only bond between the 'here-now' and the 'there-then' would be a remote temporal control.

Horatio's narrative of the doings of Hamlet I makes that dead king a martial hero if ever there was one. Armed *Cap a pe*, he, who was, *is*. The placing of this narrative deposit in a dramatic context, at this precise point, puts that 'there-then' background into a peculiar relationship with the 'here-now' foreground*. The gap between the present and past is so narrowed indeed that the heroic out-sized martial past will continue to shadow and invade the 'here-now', i.e. what we are going to see. Study this Expository Inset closely and it is difficult not to feel that the spiritual, if not the fleshly, son of Hamlet I is not Fortinbras II who

> Of unimproved Mettle, hot and full,
> Hath in the skirts of Norway, heere and there,
> Shark'd up a List of Landlesse Resolutes,
> For Foode and Diet, to some Enterprize
> That hath a stomcke in't:

and that the "dying voice" of Hamlet does not fall on him justly. If this is so, then this Expository Inset does much more than give the theatre-audience some facts for their understanding of the play. In driving a column to obtain a perspective, it points to the heart of the matter. For the Ghost re-enters after both stage- and theatre-audience are made anxious about the external military threat to Denmark. It is the menace of a Norwegian invasion which is

> the cheefe head
> Of this post-hast, and Romage in the Land,

but the Ghost's prompt re-appearance draws together, if not fuses, the historical background and the action in the foreground in an instant. This connection is relaxed when the Ghost, declaring himself at last to Hamlet, shows no concern for the defence of his realm against the Norwegians but instead an exclusive interest in his death, sufferings in purgatory and his revenge.

2. INTERIOR PLOT-REQUIRED INSET

Ophelia's narration to Polonius of Lord Hamlet's "ungartred" appearance in her chamber has been touched on earlier†, so

---

* I refer to the diplomatic and military activities of the play. When Hamlet I re-appears after Act I, whether represented by the Player King or again as the Ghost, his interests and anxieties are less martial than domestic.

† See above pp. 7–9.

that we will here consider, under this head, the narrative of Ophelia's drowning.

Certainly, once Shakespeare had chosen death by drowning for Ophelia—influenced, it has been suggested, by an inquest on a girl who had either been drowned or had drowned herself in the Warwickshire Avon—he was obliged to tell it and not show it. Even the Elizabethan theatre could not have a river on the stage despite the First Gravedigger's later efforts. (A number of characters drown in Shakespeare, and there is a vast array of references to drowning—enough to suggest a childish phobia of the river—but no drowning is actually shown.) Having chosen drowning for Ophelia, he made a nice choice because—in the absence of witnesses*—it would have been difficult for a coroner's jury to return other than an open verdict. Yet the jury returned a verdict of *felo de se*. By choosing drowning for Ophelia, Shakespeare chose the mode of death which would be precisely open to the First Gravedigger's laying down of the law—*se offendendo*, etc.—in the following scene. But how did the clumsy and wit-disordered girl, all got up with flowers, come to be clambering on the weak branch of a willow that hung "aslant a Brooke"?

Leaving that question aside, and accepting that the drowning could not be shown, we can agree that the Queen's account of Ophelia's death to Laertes, her brother, was strategically timed. What Claudius says after the recital:

> Let's follow, Gertrude:
> How much I had to doe to calme his rage?
> Now feare I this will give it start againe;

might make this seem doubtful. Against that, he shows no astonishment at the news of Ophelia's death. He knew about it before. The "How sweet Queen?" as Gertrude entered, was probably disingenuous, an interruption arranged between the spouses before the King interviewed Laertes.

The decision to narrate Ophelia's death, consequent on choosing drowning, ensures a remarkable discordance between the actual picture the spectators see and the words which the

---

* Yet there had either been an eye-witness, sub-poenaed at the inquest, who could not swim and whose evidence the Queen had remembered; or the Queen had deduced—if not fancied—remarkably well.

audience hear, words which create for them an imaginative picture utterly different from the actual picture of a castle interior.

The Queen's narrative of the accidental or suicidal drowning of Ophelia, beginning

> There is a Willow growes aslant a Brooke,
> That shewes his hore leaves in the glassie streame:
> There with fantasticke Garlands did she come,
> Of Crow-flowers, Nettles, Daysies, and long Purples,
> That liberall Shepheards give a grosser name;

has a lyrical pulse—accentuated by the half or para-rhymes streame/come/name—and a melodic movement that distinguishes the passage from the verse of the urgent give-and-take, the dramatic here-and-now, in which it is set. The movement of the first line is reminiscent of the movement of the opening of an Inset in *A Midsummer Night's Dream*, "I know a banke where the wilde time blowes"*. Now the effect of this lyrical movement is to impose a truce on the thrust and parry of the dialogue. Abstracting the stage-audience from their *present*, their is-ness, abstracting them from friendly quarrel or querulous friendship (Claudius and Laertes draw together only because they have both been wronged by Hamlet), by translating them to another, though recent, time and to another, though presumably nearby, place, the Queen thereby—and simultaneously—abstracts the theatre-audience from their involvement in the critical moment of the *here*. She does this by interposing a lyrical narrative (or narrative lyric) which makes her stage-audience a captive audience, unable to interrupt. And this is a great feat on Gertrude's (and Shakespeare's) part because the narrator can hardly enact the substance of her narrative lyric in illustration. Gertrude might, as the centre of attention, and in stage-practice generally does, spread wide her arms as she describes, not the spreading arms of Ophelia, but her spreading clothes in the lines

> Fell in the weeping Brooke, her cloathes spred wide,
> And Mermaid-like, a while they bore her up,

but she could hardly imitate the actions of the heroine of her

* Though the rhymes in that Inset are more insistent and regular.

narrative lyric in the preceding passage:

> There on the pendant boughes, her Coronet weeds
> Clambring to hang; an envious sliver broke,
> When downe the weedy Trophies, and her selfe,
> Fell in the weeping Brooke*.

Nevertheless, able to effectively enact—or simply suggest—the clumsy daft-for-love and daft-for-death girl's movements or not, Gertrude does impose this interregnum (whether or no it has been studied and rehearsed) in the temporal-spatial present. She does so by a careful choice of verbs. At the start of her poem, the willow 'growes' and the same tree 'shewes' (internal rhyme) its reflection. These mark a present which will continue beyond the literal catastrophe she has to narrate and are of the same order as the opening verbs in "I knowe a banke where the wild time blowes". But they are followed by a change of tense enforcing an accompanying change of vocal tone,

> There with fantasticke Garlands *did* she come.

Then follows the whole watery, floral, pathetic story framed by that 'did'. Still, Gertrude rounds off her narrative with the lyrical movement and the lyrical rhyme with which she had begun:

> but long it could not *be*,
> Till that her garments, heavy with her drinke,
> *Pul'd* the poore wretch from her melodious lay
> To muddy death.

Then the pause. We assume, and in stage practice we get, a long pause before the here-now is resumed with Laertes' laughable question

> Alas then, is she drown'd?

and the Queen's laughable confirmation

> Drown'd, drown'd.

Laughable, because the fact that Ophelia is drowned has been the point of the Queen's story all along, but the question of

---

* The rhyme or para-rhyme continues, and is here internal: *broke/Brooke*.

Laertes is necessary since the fact has been so softened by the lyrical 'beauty' of the Queen's poem that both the stage- and the theatre-audience need to be assured, to have it straight and short. But with Laertes' question the spell is broken and the dramatic here-and-now is resumed.

However authentic, in the view of the Coroner at the inquest on Ophelia's body, the Inset of Gertrude—purporting to be an eye-witness account—may be, it has an acute poetic relevance to Ophelia's last live appearance on the stage. In that appearance (IV. v.) she had had a lot of real or imagined flowers which she had distributed to a stage-audience, had been probably fantastically garlanded*, and had sung pretty 'country' songs at once melodious and obscene—songs full of *doubles entendres* of which the singer had been unaware. This points the connection between one kind of Inset and another in *Hamlet*. Ophelia's drowning had, because the theatre is not a cinema, to be narrated and not shown; but Shakespeare, having decided that, gave Ophelia a flowery and a swanlike end, dying in music. The policy made for consistency with respect to poor Ophelia's nature, but it also ensured the communication of the different Insets at depth. At a perspective remoter than the physically visible scene there is a connection between Gertrude's Inset in IV. vi. and the earlier Insets that are Ophelia's songs.

3. PLAY WITHIN PLAY: *The Murder of Gonzago*

The play of *Hamlet* contains, like *Love's Labour's Lost* and *A Midsummer Night's Dream*, an Inset play. In *Love's Labour's Lost* and *A Midsummer Night's Dream* professional players pretend they are amateur players; in *Hamlet* professional players act the parts of professional players. The distinction has an important consequence: in *Love's Labour's Lost* and *A Midsummer Night's Dream* the stage-audience intervenes between the theatre-audience and the Inset players to point out that these Inset players *are* amateurs. The stage-audience, in the two comedies, are amused when they should be moved by the tragedy of *Pyramus and Thisbe* and are untouched by the

---

* She always is in stage-practice, though there is no explicit stage-direction.

pathetic realization that the Nine Worthies are dead and gone. These two stage-audiences, their consciences uncaught, do not simply intervene between the homely amateurs and theatre-audience; rather they teach the theatre-audience how to mock the well-intentioned but clumsy and pretentious efforts of conceited exhibitionists. Their patronizing criticism, however, goes so far that the eventual rebukes they receive from Holofernes or Quince arouse the sympathy of the theatre-audiences. But these rebukes come near the end of both entertainments. Until the rebukes are administered (bringing about a reversal of feeling when merited teasing is carried too far*) we—the theatre-audience—also amuse ourselves at the expense of the Inset actors.

In the case of 'The Murder of Gonzago' the situation is otherwise. These professional actors are not mocked by the courtly stage-audience even though one of that audience, Polonius, is an experienced amateur actor, and another, Hamlet, is a dramatic critic of a high order as well as a dramatist (at least in collaboration) and something of a producer. The members of the stage-audience at the playing of 'The Murder of Gonzago' do not mock; they are impressed. Nevertheless they are not so spell-bound as to be silent. They do pass comments, critical among others, but only one of these comments is at all like those passed by the facetious or snobbish audiences at the courts of the Duke of Athens or the King of Navarre, and that is Gertrude's

The Lady protests too much me thinkes.

But, considered, this remark is less like an adjudicator's criticism of an actress at an Amateur Drama Festival than a criticism of the text, a criticism based on the critic's knowledge of psychological probability, of feminine nature. As such the remark tells not against the professional actors but against herself, and it is taken up, not by the actors, but by another member of the stage-audience, Hamlet. Indeed, this distinguishes the behaviour of the audience at the Court of Elsinore—

---

* Shakespeare is supreme in creating this kind of reversal. Consider the cases of Shylock and Malvolio. Prospero himself tormented his enemies until his heart relented and he reversed—to forgive.

their remarks do not affect the actors on the stage. This Elsinore audience, with the exception of Hamlet—who was part playwright and producer of the scenes in progress, and who is therefore, even on these grounds alone, especially interested—forms a closed circuit. Their comments are aimed not at the performers (as was the case at Athens and in *Love's Labour's Lost*) but against each other—that is, until Hamlet bridges the distance between professional actors and their audience by directly accosting the player of Lucianus with

Begin Murderer. Pox, leave thy damnable Faces, and begin.

How was this play within a play staged? With the tragedy of Pyramus and Thisbe and the Pageant of 'the Nine Worthies' we cannot exactly determine and the suggestion that both *Love's Labour's Lost* and *A Midsummer Night's Dream* were probably designed for performance in the hall of a Great House does not help since we do not know the architecture of that hall. Even so, it is likely that the traditional manner of presenting the 'play-within-the-play' up-stage and elevated on some sort of platform, with the stage-audience ranged down-stage towards both wings is correct. The professional actors playing the parts of amateur actors, who have most to say, then confront the theatre-audience and the impression they create is filtered through the stage- or inner-audience to those in the main auditorium. The perspectives are established in this way.

In the case of 'The Murder of Gonzago' the staging would hardly have been different. That 'The Murder of Gonzago' took place in the 'study' or inner-stage of the public theatre, a framed recess of some kind, is suggested by the scenario of the dumb show in F1 and Q2, and is supported by the stage-direction in Q1, a text which is, of course, in some respects nearer to the immediate reality of a contemporary (or late Elizabethan) performance than either F1 or Q2. The stage-direction in Q1 reads

Enter in a Dumbe Shew, the King and the Queene, he sits downe in an Arbor, *she leaves him: Then enters Lucianus with poyson in a Viall, and powres it in his eares, and goes away: Then the Queene commeth and findes him dead: and goes away with the other.*

This direction, in a bad Quarto, or stolen text, is a dishonest actor's or reporter's account of what actually did happen in 1602 or 1603; and that "arbor" points to a *mise-en-scène* which had been prepared behind the curtain temporarily masking the inner-stage. In that "arbor" there was presumably a theatrical "bank" prepared on which the Player King stretched out to sleep.

That "arbor" reminds us of the "arbor" in which, first in 1589 but often in revivals thereafter, Hieronymo's son, Horatio, was hanged. That hanging must have taken place in an inner-stage (which also represented an "arbor") because the player of Horatio had to have a form to stand on and that bench would have to be masked by a property "bank". Horatio was hanged from a tree and that tree would have to be carefully set behind a curtain in advance. When the curtains were drawn back, the inner-stage would represent very well an arbour or bower— an out-of-doors recess (designed for recreation or love-play*), its opening confronting the audience, its suspended occupant confronting Hieronymo and Isabella on the main platform-stage.

Now there is of course a series of connections between *Hamlet* and *The Spanish Tragedy*. To recollect two of these links: Belleforest's *Saxo-Grammaticus* provided a source for both plays and Kyd had also composed a 'Hamlet' (indeed portions of the dialogue of 'The Murder of Gonzago' in Shakespeare's *Hamlet* may include or echo lines in the equivalent scene in Kyd's 'Hamlet'). Moreover, *The Spanish Tragedy* had been revived, with some superbly fine additions by an unknown hand, as recently as 1602—within twelve months of the première of *Hamlet*. The connection between the two Revenge plays, and the hero who was out to avenge his murdered son and the hero who was out to avenge his murdered father, would have been clear to those Elizabethans who comprised the audience at both plays. Certainly many who had seen the première of *The Spanish Tragedy* would see the 1602 revival, and the resemblances between the two plays, and, no less, the

---

* "This place was made for pleasure, not for death", remarks Hieronymo who is indignant that the hanging should be done "in *my* bower". *The Spanish Tragedy*, II.v.11-12.

differences (each of the plays mirroring the other), would charge the experience with excitement*.

It might be sensibly contended that the more profitable parallel to draw here would be that between the 'Tragedy of Soliman' and 'The Murder of Gonzago' than that between the latter and the scene showing the hanging of Horatio. One is forced to recognize that the 'play-within-the-play' in *The Spanish Tragedy* was in the minds of the theatre-audience of *Hamlet* while they watched 'The Murder of Gonzago'. It is exceedingly improbable that the 'Tragedy of Soliman' was played anywhere but in the same inner-stage which had earlier represented the "arbor" and where Horatio had been 'hanged'. Of course there is a close relation between the two 'plays-within-the-play' scenes, but just as close, with respect to certain imaginative essences and visual properties, is, minding the common pictorial representation of an 'arbor' *in depth* as a setting for a murder, the relation between 'The Murder of Gonzago' and the 'hanging of Horatio'. In any case, both scenes in *The Spanish Tragedy* are in long perspective. They provide recessional pictures, and it is here just to recall that it was Kyd—Kyd precisely and not Marlowe—who had the theatrical flair and the appreciation of pictorial effects which made him the pioneer investigator of most of those methods of 'Inset' which are the subject of this essay.

In whatever way the 'Pageant of the Nine Worthies' or 'Pyramus and Thisbe' or, come to that, 'The Dumbe Shew' in *Pericles*, were performed, it is then pretty obvious from the nature of the evidence and of theatrical tradition, even if the text itself in isolation did not proclaim it, that *Hamlet's* 'play-within-a-play' was mounted centre and up-stage—so far up-stage in fact as to take place in that recess or curtained box known as the inner-stage; and that the stage-, inner-, or Court-audience had seats by the wings of the main forward platform. Tradition has it that Hamlet, with his head in Ophelia's lap for some of the time (producers assume that his request is granted), is positioned *down right* and it is from there that he watches the throned Claudius *down left*. Theatre practice has it

---

* *The Spanish Tragedy* had originally antedated *Hamlet* by twelve or fifteen years, but the additions to the text for the 1602 revival suggests the unknown author's full consciousness of *Hamlet*.

thus if only because this deposition is most effective, and convenient for all concerned, and that is the final justification.

So, then, the theatre-audience and spectators hear and watch 'The Murder of Gonzago' by way of the hearing and seeing of another audience on the stage. To that theatre-audience two planes are presented in visual perspective, and these two planes correspond with two orders of reality. The players in 'The Murder of Gonzago'—professional actors playing the parts of professional actors in the exercise of their craft—necessarily adopt a heightened, an exaggerated, mode of declamation on their remote stage. This style of delivery is needed so that it will be distinguished from the comparatively naturalistic interjections of the stage-audience; it is in fact also demanded by the rhetoric of their lines and by their stilted and emphatic couplet rhymes. Their movements are similarly deliberately histrionic—stately, formal, ritualistic*. And these movements are performed *twice*. The professional players first perform them in a 'dumbe shew' and, while 'hoboyes play', slowly, and as gravely and explicitly as members of a charade (since, at this point, there are no accompanying words) their movements are charged with the task of making all plain. They mime in a lighted recess:

Enter a King and Queene, very lovingly: the Queene embracing him. She kneeles, and makes shew of Protestation unto him. He takes her up, and declines his head upon her neck. Layes him downe upon a Banke of Flowers. She seeing him a-sleepe, leaves him. Anon comes in a Fellow, takes off his Crowne, kisses it, and powres poyson in the Kings eares, and Exits. The Queene returnes, findes the King dead, and makes passionate Action. The Poysoner, with some two or three Mutes comes in againe, seeming to lament with her. The dead body is carried away: The Poysoner Wooes the Queene with Gifts, she seemes loath and unwilling awhile, but in the end accepts his love.

Exuent.

* Harry Levin in 'An Explication of the Player's Speech' (*The Question of* Hamlet, 1959, pp. 141–164) well remarks that "since the theater perforce exaggerates . . . it takes a specially marked degree of amplification and stylization to dramatize the theatrical" and adds that "the contrasting textures of the Player's fustian and Hamlet's lines, like the structural contrast between the prevailing blank verse and the rhyming couplets of the play-within-the-play, bring out the realities of the situation by exposing its theatricalities." Levin is here considering—as I am—the effects of a double audience.

Thus the Folio text. Quartos 2, 3 and 4 do not significantly vary the 'business' and agree that the bank has 'flowers'.

The stage direction of the pirated Quarto 1 is more concise. It omits the Folio's piece about the Queen's show of endearments and homage, the poisoner's kissing of the crown, the Queen's "passionate action" and the entry and behaviour of the 'Mutes', but it prescribes the essentials. Either the pirate's line of sight was not good enough—if he were an actor standing in the wings, or if he were stationed anywhere except in the centre of the auditorium, this is understandable enough—to observe these studied refinements of production or he assumed that the actors in the Dumbe Shew had developed *ad lib* from hints contained in the scenario. What Quarto 1 does insist on is that the Dumbe Shew (and therefore no less the following re-play with words) takes place in an Arbor—that is, the inner stage.

As Quince's prologue to the tragedy of 'Pyramus and Thisbe' tells all so this Dumbe Shew is so much more than a trailer. Hamlet has devised the scenario of the Dumbe Shew to re-present the poisoning of his father and the easy transference of his mother's love from first to second husband. These crimes will be reconstructed according to the details released by the Ghost or inferred by his son. But of course there is a formalization. The pouring of poison from a vial* into King Hamlet's (or Gonzago's or Albertus') ears is naturalistic, but the Queen's endearments and homage and her wooing by the Poisoner are ceremonial. An attitude professed over years in the case of the first, an activity prosecuted for nearly two months in the case of the second, are formally compressed. Similarly, the poisoner's kissing of the crown is not naturalistic but emblematic. Elaborate as it is, the Shew is wholly ceremonial except at its crisis—the act of poisoning. (Referring back to the Ghost's speech in I. v., telling how he was murdered upon his 'secure hour' in the orchard, we find that death by poison was the only time-located fact disclosed—that and the fact of the wooing with "gifts"†.) The representation of the poisoning in III. ii.

---

* The stage direction of Q1, though not of F1, establishes this item of hand-property.

† cp. "Oh wicked Wit, and Gifts, that have the power/So to seduce" (I. v.) with "The Poysoner Wooes the Queene with Gifts" (s.d. III. ii.).

occupies just about the same measure of time as the original deed of poisoning as narrated by the Ghost but all else is emblematic (e.g. the kissing of the crown) or ceremonial (e.g. the wooing with gifts). Poor Claudius is obliged to suffer the re-enactment of his villainy twice—once without words and once with. He finds the play past enduring when for the second time he is made to witness poison being poured into ears— but that is *because* it is the second time.

If there had been no preliminary 'Dumbe Shew', Claudius could have sat it out in the protective semi-darkness and not have risen and cried out for "some Light". But because the movements of a dumb show have to be so unnaturally outsized, because the gestures of mime have to be so grotesquely obvious and unrealistically exaggerated (since without any assistance from words the movements and gestures must, as it were, 'shout' in themselves), an event that might have been over-looked by an audience—even a member with a guilty con-science might hope or assume the event to be overlooked by the rest of the audience—is hideously extended. The dripping of the poison into ears might have taken no longer in representa-tion than in actuality, but the outsize "viall" marked 'poison', the outsize gesture of shaking the liquid in its container, the gesture of uncorking—well, these movements are done more slowly and with far larger flourishes than is permissible or possible when there is an accompanying dialogue. Claudius, almost before a word is said, is softened up by being made to see the equivalent of a *slow-motion* film of his crime. Yet the Players will not keep counsel and after showing it they next proceed to tell all. The slow-motion film has now a sound-track and the action is consequently speeded up to approach the normal (not to attain it, there is a difference of rhetoric— with an accompanying difference between the Players' deliberately histrionic and the usual gestures demanded by Shakespearean verse of the characters, between the play-within-the-play and the play, between the Senecan 'Murder of Gonzago' and Shakespeare's *Hamlet*), but, to Claudius, all has been disclosed by the slow-motion film of the poisoning. If only *that* is not repeated he could still sit it out in the semi-darkness and enquire about the authorship later. But it is repeated, and precisely at that point the sound-track stops and Lucianus reverts to the outsize flourishings and unstoppering of the vial. Probably the vial is gigantic too. But for the magnification of these proceedings, Claudius could have endured.

This much is certain: each detail of the Players' performance in 'The Murder of Gonzago' is appallingly clear to Claudius; it is necessary therefore that each detail should be equally clear to the theatre-audience so that its impact on Claudius is realized. How was this achieved, remembering the distance of the Elizabethan inner-stage from the auditorium? The deployment of the stage-audience, converging towards the entrance to the 'Arbor' and their concentration would have worked as a funnel for directing the focus of the theatre-audience.

*　　*　　*

Here then is an Inset of a different character and intensity from the Masque of the Nine Worthies in *Love's Labour's Lost* or the tragedy of Pyramus and Thisbe in *The Midsummer Night's Dream*. The plays-within-the-plays in the two comedies were both historical, were recessions in time and each had a communication with their contexts or frames. But the communication between Inset play and its surround is more direct and more complex in *Hamlet*. The 'Nine Worthies' does not tell on Navarre, though it may tell on the pathos of Fame "that all seek after in their lives"; and 'Pyramus and Thisbe' tells on the lunacy of lovers but not especially on the lunacy of those watching. But Claudius is made to rub his nose in it—and the 'it' is his past and the origin of the play's action. As with other Insets, a stage-audience is here captured and made inert while a theatre-audience sees and hears through them, but both the audience **in** *Hamlet* and the audience **of** *Hamlet* are in a different order of relation to the show put on for them. The *Hamlet* play shows, as through a window in a recess, that part of the past which Hamlet has been bidden to remember so that he will, in the future, revenge. The watching Claudius is made to remember and so fear for his future. The Inset play translates into other terms (dramatic, the present tense, the first person) the narrative Inset of the Ghost in I. v. Narrative and dramatic Insets corroborate each other. They fuse at some point in the hinterland behind the closed room of Elsinore Castle, but advance to engage with the here and now. Not only does one other time and place combine with the present of the Players' performance: "the Story is extant and writ in choyce Italian".

4. THE SONG INSET

In *Hamlet* IV. v., 'Elsinore: a room in the Castle', as editors agree, Ophelia makes two appearances. On each occasion she sings "snatches of old tunes"*. These songs would nowadays be called folk-songs; in Shakespeare's time they would more likely be called 'country songs' for they are about country matters—copulation, jilting or maid-betrayal, death. It was just such songs that Ophelia was still singing when, after the willow-bough had broken beneath her, she was "Pulled from her melodious lay" to "muddy death".

We may take it that Shakespeare's contribution to the authorship of Ophelia's country-songs was negligible or nil, that he had nothing to do with the "old tunes", but that his contribution consisted precisely in the *placing* of the songs in this scene—incidentally preserving them from oblivion. Further, he selected from the whole body of country-song just those fragments or "snatches" which, placed where they are placed, transform the bawdy and comic into innocent—even naive—poignancy. Thus

> By gis, and by S. Charity,
> Alacke, and fie for shame:
> Yong men wil doo't, if they come too't,
> By Cocke they are too blame.

is honest country-wisdom, the lines codifying what generations of village elders would have remarked—whether the "By Cocke" is a substitute for the forbidden "By God!" or whether it refers to the bodily instrument by which the young men are to blame. The lines sung from the village ale-house bench are comic, wise and true. But the continuation

> Quoth she before you tumbled me,
> You promis'd me to Wed:
> So would I ha done by yonder Sunne,
> And thou hadst not come to my bed.

* Q. I has the stage direction, "Enter Ophelia playing a Lute, and her haire downe singing."

marks a change of approach and of voice. The general warning about the ways of young men is to be illustrated by an example: that being so, it is a sufferer (who did not take the warning to heart) who complains in person. Plaintively, this 'I' tells how she was deceived by a promise to wed and was undone. Now why does Ophelia sing these lines? Does she identify herself with the 'she-I' of the song? Had Prince Hamlet in fact—and despite the severe warnings that the "greene Girle" had received from her finger-wagging father—got her with child on 'promise' of a marriage? Or perhaps the warnings had been administered when it was already too late? We can never tell (the 'crowner' who 'sat' on the corpse did not order an autopsy), but I think that, balancing the probabilities, he had, or that Ophelia, whose mind was 'greener' than her body and yet not completely 'green', thought he had*. Two matters occupy Ophelia's snatches of "old tunes"—death and a jilting. Combinedly, it might be said, the two matters propel Ophelia into that clumsy climb along that branch over-hanging the river. The death of her old father from the hands of the "young man" would be a blow at first (with, on reflection, some relief since she would not have to confess her plight to him), but still not so dismaying as the awful knowledge if her father's murderer was the father of a child she was carrying. Nor did it seem likely that she might become Queen of Denmark as a consolation—an abundantly satisfying one. Goe to!—she was a "greene Girle" and *therefore* pathetic. The country-song, which one would have expected to be heard sung merrily enough

* The dialogue in III. ii.
    Oph.   You are keene my Lord, you are keene.
    Ham.   It would cost you a groaning, to take off my edge.
    Oph.   Still better and worse.
    Ham.   So you mistake Husbands.
shows that Ophelia can follow, if not counter, bawdy. To assume that she had taken off Hamlet's "edge" in the belief that this would secure him as a husband is perhaps to go further than this passage warrants. The assumption might indeed be dismissed as a Bradleian conjecture. We cannot of course be sure that Ophelia was pregnant (or non-pregnant), but in Shakespeare's day, as in ours, many brides were *enceinte* when marriage vows were exchanged, and with even less reproach than in ours. Still, some girls could "mistake" and become disappointed. My suggestion is the obvious one and it must have been made before—though not by a mind as noble as Bradley's.

round the ale-house fire, becomes poignant because of its application to Ophelia herself—an application which the theatre-audience ought to perceive although her stage-audience, consisting of Horatio, Gertrude and Claudius, do not.

During her second appearance in this same scene, Ophelia has an addition to her audience in Laertes. And she changes her tune:

> And will he not come againe,
> And will he not come againe:
> No, no, he is dead, go to thy Death-bed,
> He never wil come againe.
> His Beard as white as Snow,
> All Flaxen was his Pole:
> He is gone, he is gone, and we cast away mone,
> Gramercy on his Soule.

The subject of her country-song is not now seduction by a young man and his troth-break but the death of an old one. If her first song was a covert—covert because disguised under the impersonality of a folk-song—revelation to the kith and kin of young Lord Hamlet, then this second song is a hint to Laertes, the son of her killed father, Polonius. (The lines of the old song clearly indicate to a producer the kind of wig and beard to be worn by the player of Polonius: he is to be presented as an old man with pale yellow hair and a white beard.) If, 'Note this, your son, nephew and friend has treated me so', is the message (not received) of the first song, then, 'Note this, Laertes, I have had to endure the death of our father while you have been gadding in Paris and that event has put me in this state', is her message (not received) of the second (though Claudius will see to it that this message is received later). These are the 'messages' of Ophelia's two major songs, but they are respectively pointed or distance-signalled by her two snatches following almost immediately on her first entry. Thus

> How should I your true love know from another one?
> By his Cockle hat and staffe, and his Sandal shoone.

points to the major song on the theme of seduction and desertion (though Gertrude, who will not register this charge against her son's honour or discretion, responds with "Alas sweet Lady: what imports this Song?"); while

> He is dead and gone Lady, he is dead and gone,
> At his head a grasse-greene Turfe, at his heeles a stone.

points to the major song on the theme of father-murder (whereon Gertrude protests "Nay but Ophelia", but cannot justly pretend innocence since she was present at the killing). There is method in Ophelia's madness although it is to the advantage of Gertrude to pretend there is none on one score and to the advantage of Claudius to pretend there is some on the other.

As in the case of *Twelfth Night*, II. iv. (where Feste's "old and antique song", though seemingly referring to all despairing wooers has particular reference to the despairing Orsino), so the songs of Ophelia are given a specialized and poignant relevance to the situation of their singer. But like other Insets they impose on the stage-audience the frozen attitudes of passive reception. The dialogue between the songs or snatches punctuates Ophelia's recital with some feeble movement but, in general in this scene, the figures of the stage-audience become fixed and motionless in the view of the theatre-audience. Ophelia thereby attains an authority she is unlikely to have ever commanded before. This authority is only possible because, in this scene, she is able to unite her own frail person and her own doubly pathetic case to the 'standard' pathetic case of all girls who 'gave' themselves on an unhonoured promise of marriage, and of all father-bereaved wenches. Their plights have been expressed in the forms of gnomic verses and traditional song. Since these songs issued from an overwhelmingly rural society they are themselves rural. Attaching these songs to her own case, it is appropriate that Ophelia (hitherto such a little courtier) next drowns herself in idyllically rural surroundings. Thus it is Ophelia—through her songs and through the setting of her death—who gives to the Court of *Hamlet* a pastoral background. Ophelia's songs and her death endow the castle of Elsinore with a watered landscape inhabited by peasants who transmit the wisdom gained from the experience of many generations.

It will be noted that Act IV. sc. iv. of *Hamlet* is similar to *fourth act* scenes in other Shakespearean tragedies or near-tragedies. *Julius Caesar*, IV. iii. (Lucius' music), *Othello*, IV. iii. (Desdemona's song), *Cymbeline*, IV. ii. ("Feare no more the heate o' th' Sun"), *The Winter's Tale*, IV. iv. and *The Tempest*, IV. i. (the Masque scene) all provide suspensions of the plot. During each of these suspensions a song, "old and antique", stills the characters composing the picture on the stage, and creates for this picture a rural background. Practical motives may possibly have determined these Act IV Insets—such as the need to give the protagonist, or any other physically energetic male character, a breather before his violent exertions in Act V; or the need to make Act V battles or duelling the more spectacular by their contrast with a preceding lull. Whatever the motive, which may have been Shakespeare's intuitive pursuit of his form, as much or more than any respect for actors' needs, the result of these Act Four scenes is to create Insets that are not only particularly deep but are also particularly expansive. Their effect is exactly opposite to those Act IV scenes in the Comedies—e.g. the trial scene in *The Merchant of Venice*, the rejection of Hero in the church by Claudio in *Much Ado*, the baiting of Malvolio in the madhouse in *Twelfth Night*—where the prevailing romantic setting is put into perspective by action which presses forward because of its violence and tends to occlude that setting because it threatens tragedy. Such scenes in the Comedies impinge on the spectators' minds with such urgent menace that the romantic setting, within which the play began and within which it will end, is meanwhile relegated.

* * *

Hamlet is crammed with Insets. There are good reasons why this should be so. The play is a tragedy of revenge and the mood of revenge is prospective—the revenger's sights are set on a target that will only show itself as suitable for attack at some point in the future. But the revenger is dedicated to that point in the future and so cannot accept the present; Hamlet, when he had been "the glasse of Fashion", had evidently lived in his present but he is now abstracted from it. He is also bidden by the Ghost to "remember"—and "Yes, by Heaven" Hamlet will remember—and, while remembering, he will be retrospective. His "godlike reason" therefore throughout looks both "before and after". Those same conditions which inhibit him from instant action compel him to speculate or to remember, to explore temporal Insets or even to contrive—or help to contrive —one, as in 'The Murder of Gonzago'. Hamlet's mind is the central mind of the play but, functioning as it does, it obliges the other minds to function similarly—looking "before and after". Claudius is wary and remorseful, Polonius speculative and reminiscent, Ophelia fondles her memories. Now since these people—watchful, suspicious, cautious of each other—are physically limited by the play's plot and setting, the natural means for showing their relationships is the Inset. The Inset is a corridor receding at a right angle from the plane of the picture that is presented to the theatre-audience from the stage. The imagined picture framed in that Inset can be as brilliant and detailed as is Gertrude's narrative of Ophelia's drowning, or the matter of the Inset can be resistant to delineation as when Hamlet speculates on the kind of dreams ("What dreames may come?") that may occupy "the sleepe of death". Or the content of the Inset can be physically represented as by 'The Murder of Gonzago'. All through its course, the action of *Hamlet*—because that action is throttled, its straightforward frontal plot-line is impeded—tends to explode into compensatory Insets. They are corridors retreating to an enigmatic but fascinating hinterland, often minatory or pathetic, and it is this hinterland, which builds up behind the imprisoned *Hamlet* exposed on the stage, that gives this play its depth.

IX.
Word and Picture in the Final Plays

I

IN THIS chapter there will be an attempt to apply the three pairs—each pair posing an opposition—of related concepts (concepts that we have been considering throughout) to Shakespeare's Final Plays in the hope that the application might be fruitful when these plays are considered as entities moving in time and *space*—which is exactly what they are during actual performance on the stage.

To recapitulate. The first pair is usually referred to painting, though the reference could just as well be to a natural scene or, as we shall urge, to a theatrical scene. The terms defining this opposition are *foreground* and *background*, expressing nearness as against far-ness, of 'here' as against 'there'. Since the terms 'foreground' and 'background' are opposites, they assume an intermediate 'middleground', they assume the recognition of degrees of approach and recession, of varying planes in space, and the possibility of rendering these planes in pictorial art according to the laws of perspective. In the theatre there is likewise a 'down-stage' as opposed to an 'up-stage' (and there are the in-between planes), a nearness or a far-ness with respect to the audience. In the texts of Shakespeare's plays the movement of characters within the continuum foreground/background is everywhere presumed so that when, for example, in *Hamlet*, Gertrude says "But look where sadly the poor wretch comes", it is likely that she is not on a stage-level with Hamlet as he enters, that she is likely to say this relatively down-stage on espying Hamlet entering relatively up-stage, and that she and Claudius withdraw up-stage before Hamlet encounters Polonius in the 'fore-ground'. In the texts such movement is presumed and, in the conditions of performing these texts in the theatre, a producer has constantly to mind these perspectives*. Thus in *The Winter's Tale*, I. ii., Leontes almost certainly has to watch from a position in depth (that he can only watch, not hear, precipitates the tragedy) the conversation of Hermione and Polixenes. Leontes, 'here' (foreground or down-stage); they 'there' (background or up-stage)—or *vice-versa*: removed from the audience, or in propinquity to the audience, Leontes observes those two "paddling palms" *there*.

The first pair of concepts has to do with space, with pictorial composition: a half, or, if these things cannot be measured, a great part of any Shakespeare play during actual performance is 'pictorial'.

The second pair has to do with language. Just as the eye can realize nearness as opposed to far-ness in space, can distinguish here from there, advance or recession, in picture or in natural landscape, so grammatical inflections distinguish nearness from far-ness, 'now' from 'then', advance or recession, not in space, but in time. The terms are: the 'present' as opposed to the 'past' tense. But as in painting or in stage-craft, degrees of distance from the viewer in the continuum of space are recognized by the term 'middle-ground' (or 'centre-stage'), denoting intermediacy between 'foreground' and 'background', 'down-stage' and 'up-stage', so the temporal scale is recognized. The 'past' stretches back, perhaps infinitely: very well, the language can distinguish degrees of temporal recession. Behind the 'now' of actions being presently and visibly performed are the actions which are completed or 'perfect' and, behind these, are actions performed yet more remotely in the past and these are expressed by the 'past-' or 'plu-'perfect tense. Clearly there can be correspondence or agreement between the space-time 'here/now' (foreground-present), on the one hand and the

* In this book the modern producer's terms 'up-stage' and 'down-stage' are used in default of our knowledge of the Elizabethan producer's standard equivalents. In the Elizabethan public theatre, the existence of a tarras, or upper stage, meant that there was another dimension—the vertical—forming part of the pictorial composition. But this dimension is certainly presumed in only some of Shakespeare's texts, in others doubtfully, and in others not at all.

space-time 'there/then' (background-past perfect) on the other; but, intermediate between these, a 'middle-ground' (neither really here and now nor there and then) can correspond with the simple past tense.

The third pair has also, indeed, to do with language, but is less obviously concerned with language than with literary forms, or kinds. The opposition is the grand one between 'narrative' and 'drama'. They are opposed in that the narrative is tackled in the perfect (and past-perfect) tense. The story-teller employs the third-person pronouns 'he' or 'she' or 'they'; he takes it for granted that, even if 'he' and 'she' are now happily living 'ever after', his persons' actions have been perfected (actions producing this abiding felicity), perhaps long perfected, before his telling. It is the case of 'once upon a time', of a 'then' and a 'there': "Once upon a time there was a man, and his name was Leir, and he had three daughters . . .". Opposed to the narrative form is the dramatic form. The dramatist shows the minute-by-minute unfolding present. The audience hears *and* sees it happening. The persons—Leir, his three daughters—come forward, here and now, to speak, each in his own person, each as 'I'. Here is the first person singular (or plural, if Goneril and Regan collude), the person here and now, choosing and embarking on actions with results of which they *are* ignorant, and which will not be perfect (in the grammatical sense) until the end of the fifth act. In the case of the narrative we know what happened, we know at least that the action is ended before the narrator reports, and are offended if the story-teller deviates from the sanctioned, from history. In the case of the drama we live in suspense at each showing of Lear and his three daughters. In drama it is still open for them to choose differently and perhaps we hope that they will; in narrative they couldn't have. In other words, the narrative mode generally agrees with the past tense (of our second pair of terms) and the background (of the first pair); the dramatic generally agrees with the present tense and the foreground. But only generally: for in Shakespeare, as in other authors, the general alignment of foreground (here) and present tense (now) of the drama, as opposed to background (there) and past tense (then) of the narrative, can break down, and does break down as one or other member of an alignment is transposed to the other side. In no phase of

Shakespeare's career does this happen so often as in the Final Plays. To close this section with a single example. In *The Tempest*, I. i., Prospero *is* narrating to his daughter, Miranda, now aged about fifteen, a series of events which took place 'there' (Milan) and 'then' (in "the dark backward and abysm of time") twelve years ago. The foreground picture, as the audience sees it, during performance, is Prospero's island, the time—now; but, as the narrative advances, Prospero backs out of his 'present', 'recedes', and he and both the audiences (the stage-audience, Miranda, and the audience in the theatre) recede with him as that past is invoked. This is a simple instance of a non-coherence between what the audience in the theatre sees (the characters on the island now) and what they listen to (about those characters long ago and elsewhere).

II

It will be clear that Hamlet's precept to the player to "Sute the Action to the Word, the Word to the Action" so that the playing will show "the verie Age and Bodie of the Time, his forms and pressure"—whether either the "very age and body of the time" of the presentation, or of the lives of the characters, is meant—admits of exceptions as soon as remembered or past actions take the 'foreground' in place of the present business with its instantaneous accompanying gesture. The Final Plays of Shakespeare are charged with such exceptions because they are laden with memories, the memories of senior characters like Pericles, Leontes, Polixenes, Prospero. These memories can be drawn from the "dark backward" of a time long anterior to the events now to be shown on the stage, and that 'past', that 'background', variously overcast, will now exercise its power on the present foreground action. Behind *The Winter's Tale* and *The Tempest* are phantom plots which Shakespeare did not dramatize but which he narrated (indeed the drama of the earlier part of *The Winter's Tale* has the narrative begun by Polixenes' "We were as twyn'd Lambs . . ." behind it, and the latter part has Time's narrative behind it), and narrated to such purpose that, during their rendering, the 'there-then' masks, if not eclipses, the 'here-now'. The remote in time and space, paradoxically, becomes closer than the immediate in time and space.

It might be objected that the Histories are likewise always harking back, for is not Henry IV continually harassed by the memory of "gentle Richard"? But history is different from private memory and, in the case of *Henry IV*, the memory only produces an intention—to go on a crusade—an intention not realized within or without the play; the Histories provide scant satisfaction of the private wishes of characters and poetic justice is subordinate to the facts of English history. In the Tragedies memories are short—Lady Macbeth's memory of "giving suck" is used only to presently incite and, in the case of *Lear*, it needed a Gordon Bottomly to explain why Goneril and Regan were so cruel to their father*. And if Hamlet remembers his "father as he lived", or Othello the manufacture of a handkerchief, or if Antony's lieutenants remember the prowess of a champion before he surrendered to the fleshpots, in each case the reference is to a past which is not redeemed by the course of events shown in the foreground, in the action of the foreground play. In the Final Plays the memories are justified, the past marches forward and imposes a beautiful peace.

III

Pericles launched Shakespeare on to a new and experimental, albeit final, phase. Whether it is wholly Shakespeare's is a question that may never be conclusively answered. The present writer is inclined to share in the opinion that Shakespeare took over at III. ii.†. But anyone taking over any kind of work, begun by someone else and left incomplete, is bound to be affected— unless he scraps it all and starts with fresh foundations—by what he takes over, even though he is likely to alter some or much of that for which he has now assumed the responsibility. I am prepared to believe that Shakespeare not only pondered another man's *Pericles*, I. i. to III. i. inclusive, but that he made it his own—as second-hand clothes *can* be made one's own not only "with the aid of use" but after a shortening here or a lengthening there. Shakespeare's *Pericles* inaugurates a new phase in that it, *The Winter's Tale* and *The Tempest* not only

* In his play *King Lear's Wife*.

† But a case for Shakespeare's total authorship is presented by G. Wilson Knight with force and clarity in *The Crown of Life*, chapter II.

dramatize the relations between generations, between parents and their children, but also dramatize the effect of parents' memories on those relations; and this differentiates the plays of the final period from *Lear* or even from *Henry IV*. By 'parents' memories' we mean their experience (Leontes', Polixenes', Prospero's) and experience is something which can only be acquired in the past. By making the past or background of the the parents active in the present or foreground of their children, in the plot machinery of these plays, Shakespeare had to utilize, in terms of stagecraft and language, novel spatial and temporal perspectives. The novel conditions of Blackfriars probably favoured this experimentation. Nevertheless, the first compulsion to experiment came with this takeover of an unknown playwright's *Pericles*, I. i. to III. i. inclusive (the unknown playwright might have continued beyond III. i., but was still taken over at this point). Shakespeare, greatest of geniuses, was, one suspects, a naturally lazy man (he could "Waile his deare times waste"), was a poet who required the shock or stimulus provided by the example of a competitor disclosing possibilities, which he himself had not considered, as a condition for a new advance in his development. Jonson had administered the shock of 1597; the playwright of the abandoned (?) *Pericles*, the playwrights Beaumont and Fletcher, the prospect of having to write for the stage—and audience—of Blackfriars, together provided the shake-up of 1608–1609.

Pericles is "framed". The opening lines

> To sing a Song that old was sung,
> From ashes, auntient Gower is come,

pitch, or distance, it. Gower comes forward but only to pitch what he brings with him backwards. The opening lines pitch the "Song" not simply into the fourteenth-century, when our "auntient Gower" was not "ashes", as he is now*, but into a time which was hoary when this long-dead old man was alive, for

> *Et bonum quo Antiquius eo melius,*

---

* In the church of St. Saviour's. Nearby, the remains of Edmund Shakespeare had been buried on 31st December, 1607.

there is profit, in these "latter times", in a song that "hath been sung at Festivals" where

> Lords and Ladyes in their lives,
> Have red it for restoratives.

The "Song" of *Pericles*, from its foundations, foundations inherited by Shakespeare to build on, is not here, is not *now*, but is framed; it is remote; it is 'there/then'. Having thus framed, or placed, it in a remote perspective, Gower—and he must be down-stage to do this—tells this latter-day audience to mark the threatening aspect of Antiochus ("As yon grimme lookes do testifie"*). Despite the position of the stage-direction in the Quarto, it is evident that "Antiochus, Prince Pericles, and followers" had previously glided into the picture. Do 'Antiochus, Prince Pericles, and followers' form a tableau within the frame of an inner-stage at this point? We cannot positively know. We do know, however, that it would be difficult to present the opening of *Pericles*, whether in the disputed Globe, or the conjectural Blackfriars, or on a modern stage (supposing here a fidelity to the text), in any manner other than the one hinted. Explicitly: 'Auntient Gower', risen from the ashes, addresses a latter-day audience from down-stage in archaic English, directing them to look up-stage, to look at figures in a frame who were *there* and *then*—ashes indeed—when he (Gower) was in the flesh; to look at figures (they will presently advance down-stage and talk) in a Song, that was remote in Gower's time, when "Lords and Ladyes in their lives" (infinitely touching—those gay lords and ladies who had long been ashes when Gower was alive) "red it for restoratives". Infinitely touching! Yes, but the long perspective was established by a playwright, possibly dead himself, whose queer, abandoned, old-fashioned thing Shakespeare took up, took up to make new and modern in his own growth.

This perspective, established at the outset, whereby the audience are directed to see the old story re-enacted at a temporal and spatial remove from Gower, who was himself remote in time, tends to be modified, or shortened, between

* For an alternative interpretation, that the "grimme lookes" refer not to Antiochus' aspect but to the heads of the unsuccessful suitors, see the New Arden *Pericles*, ed. F. C. Hoeniger.

Gower's appearances: there is an alternative lengthening or shortening of focus. This is because it is the nature of drama to show a perfected action as still to come and "still unsure". Thus there is a swing in *Pericles* between Shakespeare's normal dramatic method and the method of the illustrated narrative—the dumb show or tableau in Act II is exactly such a pictorial illustration to a story. This swing did not exist in, say, *Romeo and Juliet*, for two reasons: first, the Chorus there makes fewer entrances*, does not become the expected *entr'acte* intruder and abridger of temporal gaps; and secondly, the Chorus there, far from placing affairs in the past, makes it all a 'live' issue, makes, what was medieval, renascent (i.e. modern), using present inflexions and urgently modern language in an up-to-date sonnet. Nor did it exist in *Henry V*. The Chorus in *Henry V* comes before each Act expressly to harangue and urge that what is all past is really about to happen *now*. But in *Pericles*, Gower is an *entr'acte* intruder, abridger, commentator, moralist; above all, he intrudes in order to relegate, to push or thrust back into the plu-perfect, into the 'background' (veritably, at times, the inner-stage), a quaint old story that is obstinately liable to spill forwards in time and down-stage unless Gower returns at intervals to refer it back to where it belongs—inside that frame.

So Gower relegates, and is assisted by the manner in which Act I proceeds. This manner might strike the reader as exceptionally ingenuous (reminding him of something as primitive as *Gorbuduc*), but to the 1608 playgoer it probably seemed extremely sophisticated. It is a method adapted to the remote temporal-spatial frame that has been established. This method involves the passage of elements of the plot through three tenses: Gower had told us what we were going to see dug up; next we see it (I. ii.); then (II. i.) Pericles narrates ("Attend me then, I went to Antioch") what we have just seen. What we have just seen is now projected into Pericles' past. Moreover, the whole business whereby Thaliard is employed by Antiochus to dispatch Pericles, only to find that he is too late at each station along the line to achieve his object, partakes of illustrated narrative rather than drama. A ripe dramatist, we might think, would not tell what he is to show, then show it, and then tell us

---

* None at all in the Folio text. The difference between Q1 and subsequent quartos, of the tenses of Chorus's sonnets, should be noticed.

he has shown it. To readers the first Act might appear almost a strip cartoon; surely Shakespeare could not, or, if he could, would not, at this point of his career, relapse into a dramatic method (or, rather, not a dramatic method but an illustrated narrative method) as primitive as the method of *Gorbuduc*. He probably could, and would, not initiate the method; but, having taken them over, he adopted the first two Acts and was thereafter committed, committed to explore what were (to him) novel perspectives in a kind of theatre (Blackfriars) that demanded experiment.

That the results of the experiment were successful is attested by the title page of the 1609 Quarto. *Pericles* "hath been divers and sundry times acted by his Maiesties Servants at the Globe on the Banck-side". The Globe. *Touché!* we have gone too far in presuming that Shakespeare was particularly envisaging novel conditions in Blackfriars. Accepting that *Pericles* was played in both houses, we must then additionally accept that Beaumont and Fletcher's plays, or Shakespeare's plays more particularly designed for Blackfriars, were also played in the Globe with the consequence that techniques adjusted to the conditions of the 'private' or winter house were extended to productions in the public theatre. Private theatre practice affected public theatre practice. Very well: in the setting of the Globe—and not at Blackfriars—consider the daring mixture, in Act II, of the archaic, or the affectedly archaic, with the novel temporal and spatial perspectives.

Act II begins with Gower reminding the audience of what they have seen:

> Heere have you seene a mightie King,
> His child I 'wis to incest bring.

A hoarily distant past, in which there was a riddle to which the grim answer is 'incest', lies now in the *audience's* recent past. They have *just* seen. Three degrees of 'pastness'—the audience's, auntient Gower's, and what was long past in Gower's age— are conflated. But the audience are then ordered to bide their time, "Be quiet then, as men should bee,/Till he hath past necessitie". The audience is to be patient until the old man has finished telling (the language) and showing (the pictures) his tale, but they are also referred to a future (theirs, the audience's,

yet long expired in Gower's time) when Pericles' sufferings will
be judged to have been worth while, "I'le shew you those in
troubles raigne;/Loosing a Mite, a Mountaine gaine". Stating
that this prospect is before them (a prospect that was a distant
retrospect in the speaker's lifetime), Gower immediately turns
to the stage *present,* for "the good [Pericles]/*Is* still at Tharstill",
although this present, like the future promised the audience in
that "I'le", belongs to the *Vergangenheit,* the bygone-ness, which
Gower proclaimed at the start. Yet the 'now', the present tense,
contained and announced by the lines

> *Is* still at Thastill, where each man,
> *Thinkes* all is writ, he spoken can:
> But to remember what he *does,*
> *Build* his Statue to make him glorious;

this 'is', in the order of time, becomes peremptorily withdrawn,
in the order of space when, with the couplet "But tidinges to
the contrarie,/Are brought your eyes, what need speake I", a
"Dombe shew" is introduced. The Quarto stage-direction
reads:

Enter at one dore Pericles *talking with* Cleon, *all the traine with them:
Enter at an other dore, a Gentleman with a Letter to* Pericles, Pericles
shewes the Letter to Cleon; Pericles *gives the Messenger a reward, and
Knights him: Exit* Pericles *at one dore, and* Cleon *at an other.*

What happens is that the "is" and the "thinkes" and the
"does" of Gower's language is immediately distanced, thrown
back, by the framed picture. We say "framed": it is admittedly
impossible to assert that the 'Dombe shew' took place within the
—in any case disputed—inner-stage (and perhaps, though not
certainly, the "one dore" and "an other dore" make an inner-
stage presentation unlikely), yet it is nevertheless "framed".
Gower, unless from a pedestal, can scarcely remain up-stage
and address the audience over the heads of the participants in
the 'Dombe shew'. He must either be positioned aloft in the
gallery or upper stage (but how does this accord with a Blackfriars presentation?) or, and this is the more likely, he must be
positioned 'down-stage'. Accepting the latter position, we have
Gower, from one corner or the other, addressing the audience
and referring them to a spectacle ("tidinges . . . Are brought

your eyes, what need speake I'') more remote from them in
space, set in longer perspective, than from himself. In this way
what was erstwhile 'present' has receded out and become a
framed picture; the 'now' of a moment ago has travelled into
the past. That the stage picture has wrought this effect is
evidenced by the verbs that immediately follow the 'Dombe
shew':

> Good Helicon that stayde at home, . . .
> Sav'd one of al, . . .
> How Thaliart *came* full bent with sinne,
> And *had* intent to murder him . . .

what was 'here' and 'now' a line ago—a single line plus the
irruption of the 'Dombe shew'—has become a 'there and then';
remote in time and space. Thus in one line, language, by the use
of tense inflexion, has caught up with the picture—but it
catches up so that the discordant spatial and temporal dimensions of auntient Gower's illustrated narrative become adjusted.

Nor do the daring and rapid alterations of temporal and
visual focus cease after the 'Dombe shew'. As soon as that
spectacle, set or framed in middle- or back-ground, is completed, Gower proceeds, but after another change of tense. He
now speaks of what 'had' been going on in Tyre while Pericles
'is' in Tharsis. This reference to another time and place, a
narrator's abridgement, was no doubt unavoidable. But
Shakespeare's acceptance of the challenge forced him to be
experimental, obliging him to pioneer in linguistic and pictorial
terms to project a long-term view of matters where more than
one generation was involved and where a merely tragic, or a
merely romantic-comoedic, answer would be alike unreal. The
inherited plot-line and scenario defied the Unities in extraordinary degree. (Later, Shakespeare's total acceptance, in
The Tempest, of all the Unities in answer to a challenge set by
himself or by others as a consequence of experience of, or
criticism of, *Pericles*, would also compel experiment.) Meanwhile,
the *Pericles* experiment compels Gower, after the reference to
past events at Tyre, to close the temporal gap once more:

> Good Helicon that *stayde* at home, . . .
> *Sav'd* one of all . . .
> How Thaliart *came* full bent with sinne,

> And *had* intent . . .
> He (Pericles) doing so, *put foorth* to Seas . . .
> For now the Wind *begins* to blow,
> Thunder above, and deepes below,
> *Makes* such unquiet . . .

that the storm

> *Threw* him a shore, *to give* him glad:
> And heere he *comes* . . .

and Gower retires after pointing, in these two lines, a past, a future, a present which are yet all housed in his own remote past. At his withdrawal: 'Enter Pericles wette' and, in his own person speaks, either Shakespeare's, or the indubitably Shakespearean, *Lear*-like two-and-a-half lines:

> Yet cease your ire you angry Starres of Heaven,
> Wind, Raine, and Thunder, remember earthly man
> Is but a substaunce . . .

Whether Shakespeare's lines or not, for the speech, beginning auspiciously, degenerates, Shakespeare at this point was poetically interested. And he was possibly the more interested, the more struck, if these lines were Shakespearean rather than his own, Shakespeare's. He was interested enough at this point to become committed as a poet; and, to find that his own plays, his own exercises in time and space, word and picture (to concentrate the matter on the levels of a dramatic poet's techniques), heretofore had been chastely constrained, would additionally interest. Old habit means that from III. ii. to the end there is a gradual 'close-up' as the different 'I's' speak their 'here' and 'now'. But still there are unusual departures from habitual practice, largely governed by a plot and scenario which ranged widely in space and swung backwards and forwards in time. At the conclusion, all is sealed up and distanced again by that auntient fourteenth-century poet, whose bones in Southwark Cathedral lay near the actor brother's—Edmund Shakespeare's.

And William Shakespeare's interest engaged the interest of the 1609 audience at the Globe, that Globe audience reflecting the interest of the Blackfriars audience. That audience could listen to and watch "the whole Historie, adventures, and fortunes" of Pericles, knowing that he would end successfully, because they watched and heard from a vantage position, so long after the "Lords and Ladyes" had heard the song "in their lives". The audience was fascinated (Fortuna rewards in the end, the stars are lucky), the play *Pericles* was successful, variants in scenic presentation and delivery at Blackfriars survived transference to the Globe.

IV

The dramatic poet, who had taken over, in *Pericles*, someone else's, or his own much earlier play, and made it—or re-made it in the light of twelve or fifteen years' experience—his own, and who had found—in the process of making it his own—that a plot which spanned a wide arc of time demanded novel perspectives in its showing, would have been ready to deal with Greene's *Pandosto*. Ready, even eager, for the distension asked of Shakespeare's powers in *Pericles* had been both dramatic and linguistic. Now, when sixteen years were to be covered or accounted for, a period sufficient for an infant daughter to grow to the point where she becomes nubile, memories—the pressure of the parent's past on the destiny of the child—are involved. The memories which act on the future in *Pericles*, *The Winter's Tale* and *The Tempest* are those of the father of a girl. It is as though *King Lear* were, in the Final Plays, to be made plainer by means of an autobiography of Lear and a biography of Cordelia. In the Final Plays this autobiography and the biography engage in a dialogue. The illustration of the power of the memories (either of past actions or past sufferings) of the father on the destiny of the daughter had required of Shakespeare in *Pericles* technical experiments. Technical discovery can restore, we may suppose, joy to a writer when the discovery is the instantaneous expression of an enlarged vision of life—even if the enlargement came by chance. Add therefore Blackfriars, the up-and-coming Beaumont and Fletcher, and the need somehow to harmonize word and picture when the strategy of the task, the plot, often insisted that those be at variance, and it is apparent why the test of *Pericles* should lead to *The Winter's Tale*. For they have much in common.

They have much in common but they have this difference: instead of scenes 'from the life of' Pericles, all set at a remove by Gower, *The Winter's Tale* is to be managed in two halves. Time, as the Chorus, is to apologise for, and try to bridge, between Acts III and IV, a period of time which in *Pericles* was shown at spaced intervals. But though the purpose of 'Time, the Chorus' in *The Winter's Tale* is copulative—to prevent one play becoming two plays—yet, if he succeeds in his purpose, the major consequence of his success is to place (or set) the scenes in Bohemia in a curious relation to the spectators. *If* Time succeeds, and it is a critical point whether 'he' does, then an audience, which for all of three acts has been experiencing a heady and violent *here and now*, thrusting towards its apparent satisfaction in tragedy, have to adjust their perspective and perceive the Bohemia scenes—not with the immediacy with which they perceive, or perceived, comico-tragic scenes in Shakespeare's Romantic Comedies with their temporal aura of an eternal or continuous Present tense—*but through the lens of the tragedy-determined first half*. If Time succeeds.

If Time *does* succeed—to the extent that, though they "had slept between", as Time pleads, they yet remember what had happened before they slept—the audience is confronted by a pastoral romance (IV. iv.) in Bohemia which is judged in one way by the lovers and in a very different way by themselves. Whereas Florizel and Perdita live in their 'now', in the forepeak of time, their place an everywhere—exquisite, romantic, comoedic—and see themselves as the lovers in the Romantic Comedies see themselves, the audience sees them in the light of their parents' (especially of Leontes') experience. Because he is in love, Florizel wishes, and can imagine, each moment as eternal:

> When you speake (Sweet)
> I'ld have you do it ever: When you sing,
> I'ld have you buy, and sell so: so give Almes,
> Pray so: and for the ord'ring your Affayres,
> To sing them too. When you do dance, I wish you
> A wave o'th Sea, that you might ever do
> Nothing but that: move still, still so:
> And owne no other Function. Each your doing,
> (So singular, in each particular)

157

Crownes what you are doing, in the present deeds,
That all your Actes, are Queenes.

but an audience, informed by Time of the "slide/Ore sixteene
yeres", and remembering the events of the first half of the play,
will frame these 'present deeds' and, if not distrust, yet distance
them—will project them, so that they are not accepted as all in
all, as absolute (as Florizel or Perdita in their state of euphoria
might accept them), but instead recognize them simply
('simply'—to term them 'mere' would be to speak as a complete
'square' about the central illusion of existence) as components
within a dimension of time, of a reading of life which com-
prehends the lovers' Innocence, Leontes' Experience, Leontes'
and Polixenes' age of Innocence which long antedated Perdita's
and Florizel's. The audience will take the lovers' ecstasy not at
the lovers' valuation (that their love is unique and should, and
therefore may, last for ever) but at another, and possibly higher,
valuation, knowing—as they do, if Time as Chorus has been
effective—that the lovers' moments ought indeed to be pro-
tracted infinitely (because they are priceless while they last)
but that they most certainly will *not* be under a temporal dispen-
sation which includes Age, Experience and Authority as well
as Youth, Innocence, Love. This consciousness of the audience
—at variance with the lovers' consciousness as the consciousness
of the audience was not so at variance with the lovers' consciousness in the Romantic Comedies—frames the Bohemian
pastoral romance, places it so that it is contemplated through
the lens of the lovers' parents' experience, projects it, projects
it far and away—for the Golden Age, the time of Leontes'
youth, of the audience's own youth and innocence (after what
it has lived through during the earlier Acts) are all remote*.
From within this Inset, the Shepherd, with memories of
occasions when his "old wife liv'd", and Perdita, with her mere
teenager recollections of traditional "Whitsun pastorals",
scoop—or disclose—deeper vistas†.

* Perdita's speeches, on youth and age, while distributing flowers to her
foster-father's guests, are *inspired* since she cannot have experienced what
she prattles about so sweetly. That the speeches, unknown to her, directly
touch on what the audience (who were in the theatre before she was born)
has been made to learn the hard way, is evidence of her—and Shakespeare's
—inspiration.

† See 'The Dead Wife', pp. 92 ff. above.

With Act V the Bohemian excursion ends. It has been an Inset, revealing a 'golden age' being enjoyed by Florizel and Perdita and which had once been enjoyed by their parents. The Sicilian 'here and now' returns with Act V, but until the final scene, this 'here and now' conflicts, in the audience's mind, with the Bohemian dimensions of space and time. But with Hermione's resurrection the two orders are drawn together and harmonized. When the effigy of Hermione becomes a living Hermione, and she advances from her up-stage (inner-stage?) chapel to the foreground and to a new 'here and now', then the experience of the Bohemian excursion is subsumed or incorporated.

In retrospect, it will be realized that success or failure of the play as a whole will depend, in the theatre, on the measure of conviction that Time the Chorus secured during his narrative speech. It is also, I believe, fairly evident that there would have been no *Winter's Tale* (as we know it) but for Shakespeare's previous 'take over' of *Pericles*, which resulted in a play not rudimentary in its methods but highly experimental; one which, combining as it did, narrative and drama, compelled the trying out of new visual perspectives to match the temporal scheme with its many and rapid changes of tense.

v

Whereas the action of *Pericles* straggles over the years, and the action of *The Winter's Tale* has its temporal hiatus to allow for the growth of a new generation, the visible action of *The Tempest* represents a time span scarcely greater than the time needed for its showing. Whether or not in response to criticism of its predecessors, it observes the Unities. Here, as with its two predecessors, Shakespeare chooses a plot involving a father and his daughter and, throughout its unfolding, it has points of contact with either *Pericles* or with *The Winter's Tale* or with both. All three plays end with the restoration of a father, who has been changed by his suffering, to his possessions, his fortunes, or his rights, and the happy marriage of his daughter. In all three plays the father-daughter relationship recalls some aspect of the Lear–Cordelia relationship. But with all the resemblances of story there is this main difference in tactical handling: *The Tempest*, though it supposes a period of time (here twelve instead of sixteen years) sufficient for a female infant to grow to marriageable age, renders that period, and the tragic events leading to it, entirely in narrative terms. Who can doubt that Shakespeare's choice here was partly, if not entirely, conditioned by the experience gained in the making of *Pericles* and *The Winter's Tale*? In any case, this choice obliged Prospero in I. ii. to narrate to Miranda, and through Miranda to the audience, the events of twelve years ago, and, in so doing, creating an imaginative picture which is in the strongest contrast to the actual spectacle the audience beholds. This situation was cited in the Introductory chapter above but now demands a return in the context of *Shakespeare's* situation when he composed his Final Plays. The audience sees an old man and his daughter seated side-by-side, and alone, on a luxuriant island; but, while they see this, they hear of violent, bustling, middle-of-the-night activity in which the passive victims are not—and yet, also, *are*—the Prospero and Miranda they physically behold, but rather a middle-aged Prince of Milan and a baby. Memory is powerful in Prospero while he tells Miranda the reason for the present tempest. To what extent does the picture from the past (for memories can only refer to the past) advance, obtrude upon, even super-impose itself upon, the present stage-picture offered to the audience?

Now there are three forms of expressing the perfected past in an English verb where the Latin has but one form: *amavi* may be translated as (*a*) I *loved* or (*b*) I *have loved* or (*c*) I *did love*. Grammarians differ among themselves in their use of terms, but we can call (*a*) the Simple Perfect, (*b*) the Present Perfect (since the auxiliary *have* possesses a Present inflexion and conveys a measure of its Present meaning to the past participle *loved*), and (*c*) the Emphatic Present Perfect (*did* expresses pastness but, variably according to context, emphasises the verb qualified—*love*—which has a present inflexion). Thus there is in English a choice of forms denoting a scale of remoteness or urgency within a past they all express; and at one end of the scale is a form in which the past is so re-lived in its telling that it becomes—in a manner—present. If Prospero's narration of the events which precipitated him, and his baby daughter, from Milan twelve years ago creates a picture which gradually closes up on the audience till it mingles with, even supersedes, the stage picture physically exposed to them, it is because of Shakespeare's playing on this scale—that and an earlier insistent use of the historic present and present participles. The whole of Prospero's narrative is so charged with energy, not so much because of the frequency of verbs but because of the changes of tense that the verbs undergo (contrast Egeon's narrative in *Comedy of Errors* where, despite the excitement of the events abstractly considered, there is a dead flatness of tone and monotony of tempo, unvaried perspective—all attributable to the employment of a single tensal inflection) that it demands reference to the whole of the episode to bear out the truth of these remarks. We can give here but a few examples.

From the pluperfect of half-remembrance, there is the abrupt tense-change that makes this dream-like past an 'is' that 'lives':

> *Miranda:* 'Tis farre off:
> And rather like a dreame, then an assurance
> That my remembrance warrants: *Had* I not
> Fowre, or five women once, that *tended* me?
>
> *Prospero:* Thou *hadst*; and more Miranda: But how *is* it
> That this *lives* in thy minde? . . .

Then a firm placing in the "dark-backward":

> Thy Mother *was* a peece of vertue, and
> She *said* thou *wast* my daughter; and thy father
> *Was* Duke of Millaine . . .

which "dark-backward" is to be drawn forwards in the light of these Historic Presents, Infinitives or Participles:

> he [Anthonio] *needes* will be
> Absolute Millaine . . .
> He *thinks* me now incapable. *Confederates*
> (So drie he *was* for Sway) with King of Naples
> *To give* him Annuall tribute, *doe* him homage
> *Subject* his Coronet, to his Crowne and *bend*
> The Dukedom yet *unbow'd* (alas poore Millaine)
> To most ignoble *stooping*.

So the King of Naples "*hearkens* my Brothers suit" that he "*should presently extirpate* me and mine". Whereon

> A treacherous Armie levied, one mid-night
> Fated to th' purpose, *did* Anthonio *open*
> The gates of Millaine, and ith' dead of darkenesse
> The ministers for th' purpose *hurried* thence
> Me, and thy *crying* selfe.

and, after the Present Perfect of "the very rats/Instinctively have quit it", the Present Emphatic enters in force, for the "did Anthonio open" is followed by "Wherefore did they not/ That howre destroy us?", by "to sigh/ To th' windes, whose pitty sighing backe againe/Did us but loving wrong", by "Thou was't that did preserve me; Thou didst smile", by "Gonzalo/ . . . did give us . . ." so that Miranda, experiencing the original horror consciously for the first time, can properly exclaim:

> I not remembering how I cride out then
> Will cry it ore againe:

and then—innocently enough till she learns of the names on the ship's passenger-list—turn to enquire of her father,

> And now I pray you Sir,
> For still 'tis beating in my minde; your reason
> For raysing this Sea-storme?

In *The Tempest*, Shakespeare rejected the method of illustrating a narrative at spaced intervals; equally he rejected the composition of a play in two halves. He decided in *The Tempest* to narrate the matter of most of *Pericles* and three acts of *The Winter's Tale* within much less than half of a single scene. But the decision owed much, if not all, to his experience of inheriting, or adopting, the script of an unknown playwright or of his earlier forgotten self. This inheritance, or adoption, compelled him to face the opposing claims and methods of narrative and drama, of past and present, of time and space, of language and picture (all in relation to the physical conditions of the Blackfriars Theatre as well as to the familiar ones of the Globe) and, at the last, to hit on a mode which reconciled these opposing claims as completely as possible. Looked at in this light, the interest of *Pericles* is considerable.

VI

There remains the task of considering the Betrothal Masque in *The Tempest*, IV. i. This Masque has connections with those Fourth Act scenes, with an emphasis on nature or flowers, in other later plays—*Hamlet*, *Othello*, *King Lear*, *Cymbeline*. But what more concerns us here is to note the Masque's function in the design of *The Tempest*, to compare and contrast that function with the function of IV. iv. (the Sheep Shearing Festival scene) in the design of *The Winter's Tale*, and to observe a certain similarity of mechanics.

First to point to the obvious and yet important similarities and dissimilarities. In both the Sheep Shearing Festival of *The Winter's Tale* and the Betrothal Masque in *The Tempest* there is a celebration of the fertility of the earth. In the Festival this celebration has an autumnal note; it takes place in late summer or early autumn and it recognizes the foison that has *been* given: in the Masque the blessings of

> Earths increase, foyzon plentie,
> Barnes, and Garners, never empty,

are rather *pro*spective, Juno asking that these riches should attend Ferdinand and Miranda *in their future*. Next, in the Festival, the deities Flora, Jupiter, Apollo, Dis, Phoebus, etc., though they are referred to in the dialogue, do not appear in person; in the Masque, Iris, Ceres, Juno do appear in person. In both Festival and Masque, the dramatist includes, at some point, dances in his stage-picture; in both Festival and Masque, the poet calls in the non-linguistic art of music to accompany some of the words. In both Festival and Masque, the audience sees, as an essential in the two stage-pictures, the mingling or confronting of youth and age. In both Festival and Masque, the audience is made aware, both through words and pictures, of the young lovers in their present delight and with a future before them, and of their parents' generation, burdened with remembrance, who perceive in their children a kind of re-enactment. In both scenes there is a presentation of past and future, of memory and desire.

Now, in the Festival of *The Winter's Tale*, we noted that the rapture of Florizel and Perdita is to the audience—is indeed to Polixenes—distanced or 'framed' because of the experience of the early tragic acts of the play. In *The Tempest*, no less, the Betrothal Masque (whatever its practical usefulness may have been to the poet-dramatist as a temporizer—as something to occupy ear and eye of the audience while Caliban's "foule conspiracy" gets under way) effects a change in the temporal, and probably the pictorial, perspective of the audience when it occurs. Granted that remorse or remembrance or vindictive feeling on the part of the ship's passengers or Prospero have weighed continuously on the action until the Masque, and have coloured that action, yet—with the Masque—some characters become, like ourselves, an audience, an audience within an audience. This applies to Ferdinand and Miranda; and Prospero too "had forgot" his role as character during the time he, with Ariel as a sort of Inigo Jones, is absorbed as author, producer and spectator of the Masque. During the Masque there is an escape or withdrawal from the temporal dimensions of the play's plot, an escape of the kind anyone and everyone has experienced from intense absorption—whether in a work of art, in a test match, or in anything else sufficiently compelling to participant or observer or listener.

In the Masque, the goddesses of Heaven (Juno) and earth (Ceres) and of their servant, Iris, appear or descend, and speak, and are followed by "certain Reapers" and "Nimphes" who dance. All this may be mere illusion, conjured by Prospero's "so potent Art", but it entertains Ferdinand and Miranda (for the future son-in-law is not simply flattering with his "most magestick vision"?), and it holds, as we are informed, the author-producer himself spell-bound. During the playing-time of the Masque, until it is broken off abruptly, a *time* and a *space* —other than the time and the space of the plot of *The Tempest*— are imported: imported, they occlude the time and place of the plot.

What time and what space? That belonging to the goddesses of fertility which is outside mortal first-hand experience. How was the Masque performed? And where was the inner audience of two positioned? We do not know enough about the structure of the Globe or Blackfriars, or of the winching gadgets of either, to know, or to be sure whether the audience consisting of Ferdinand and Miranda sat with their backs or their faces to the paying audience in the theatre. But, whatever the original disposition of the inner audience in relation to the divine performers of the Masque, the fact that the paying audience—whether in the Globe or in Blackfriars or in a modern theatre—beholds the Masque through the eyes of that inner audience, rather than directly, results in an adjustment of focus to correspond with the peculiar linguistic (rhyme, some octosyllabics, a special mode of heightened delivery suitable to goddesses who are putting on a show) properties of the Masque. For this method of harmonizing the pictorial with the verbal in an Inset—a deposit within a play fairly sharply demarked from its context—Shakespeare might well of course have learned something from the Court Masques and the "perspectives" of Inigo Jones. Equally well, as far as the Masque in *The Tempest* is concerned, he was profiting from the composition of *The Winter's Tale* and his recollection of the experimental *Pericles*.

X. Epilogue

I<small>N THE</small> language of literary criticism the words 'profound' or 'depth'—signifying that the poem or play (or novel) under discussion is not 'superficial' but satisfying, enriching and that it offers yet further rewards with each re-reading, re-hearing, re-watching—are so customary as not to require demonstration that such terms, or their direct equivalents in other modern European languages, are so used. A commendatory word, from Longinus to Burke and beyond, used to be 'sublime', but it is now discredited, perhaps because psychologists tell us that inspiration came to the poets not from 'above' but 'below': a poem or play nowadays had better be profound than lofty*.

Yet 'profound' like 'sublime' is a metaphor; the 'depth' is metaphorical when applied to a series of words on a page and not to lake, canal or ocean. And other words from the vocabulary of physics, fitted for ponderables and measurables, are likewise employed to convey the effect created, on those who experience literary works, by that which is strictly imponderable and immeasurable. Thus an American critic, venturing a summary judgment of American literature, says that it is wanting in "a certain density, weight and richness"†.

But one is not complaining of these metaphors. We know what 'profound' or 'weighty' (or 'elevating' or 'sublime') mean when applied to human experience and the life of the emotions, e.g. 'he felt for her a *deep* love and her loss was a *heavy* blow', and recognize their psychological truth; one can also accept them as quantitative terms expressing a reader's qualitative

* Cp. Herbert Read, "The Poet and his Muse", *Eranos-Jahrbuch*, XXXI/1962.
† Philip Rahv, *Literature in America*.

reactions to the experience of literature. They can have a more literal application to painting, where perspectives, and to sculpture, where mass, are concerned, and, still more so, to a drama while it is actually being rendered on a stage with its physical levels and dimensions.

Shakespeare, of all poets, is deep (to eighteenth-century critics, sublime), dense, weighty, enriching—yet not uniformly so: *The Taming of the Shrew* is a 'light-weight' beside *King Lear*. Every work in English is nearly a 'light-weight' weighed beside *Lear*, we might be inclined to say sometimes, but even *King Lear* is not uniformly weighty—or deep, dense and rich. On the stage, a Shakespeare play is re-enacted in physical space and time: the space refers to what the audience sees and the time to what the audience hears. There is not a constant but a varying relation, in Shakespeare, between the two dimensions and the employment, by an audience, of the two senses.

Shakespeare was a poet *and* a dramatist. Extraordinary historical, social and linguistic conditions, as well as extraordinary genius, enabled him to be completely and simultaneously both. The conditions were extraordinary, we assume, because they have never all come together to favour either poet or dramatist, still less poet *and* dramatist, so entirely since. Even so, the poet was earlier than the dramatist—this is the probability—and when the poet became a dramatist *c.* 1587–8, so that his verse was to be heard to a simultaneous visual accompaniment, there was a challenge.

How miserable the fate of the poet who could only describe (and pure poets are mainly descriptive) what could be displayed by "foure or five most vile and ragged foyles" on a platform? Not at all! The coursing of "poor Wat", the hare, could not be shown, could not be presented to the physical vision on the stage *here and now*, though it is fully realized to the imaginative vision in *Venus and Adonis*. But a hunt could be presented in *A Midsummer Night's Dream*, IV. i., *there* and now (i.e. it is taking place off-stage with suitable sound effects) or it could be described, on the stage, as having taken place there and *then*— in the past*. Shakespeare, a poet and so urged to describe as

---

* *Hippolita:* I was with Hercules and Cadmus once,
When in a Wood of Crete they bayed the Beare
With hoards of Sparta . . .

Keats was urged to describe, was driven, induced, encouraged to resort to, and develop, the device of the Inset, to practise—in his poetry—the art of temporal perspectives. But temporal perspectives could not be practised without the audience having to adjust their vision, so that they saw something more 'deeply' than they could see physically. And what the audience would then see at depth would be in varying degrees contradictory to that which was physically exposed. Nevertheless, the very day-light limitations of The Theatre and of the Globe were friendly to the device. In small-scale indeed the device was used continually (e.g. "Here lay Duncan,/His Silver skinne lac'd with his Golden Blood"), if not continuously, but it was in those crises where an audience had either to look beyond the physical scene, or to give it but secondary attention (so that this scene froze to enable the audience to look beyond more easily) that the real challenge—and opportunity—arose.

But the challenge and opportunity, the crises, would present themselves variously; the emergencies were diverse in nature. After *Henry VI* (and possibly *Richard III*) where the background would have been half-, if not fully, known to the audience, and where the dramatist could follow in the track of the Chronicles, if not a predecessor, the first emergency, in the period 1587–1590, was the need to present the background of a Comedy situation: to tell the past, the history, of people so that the growing *now* of *The Comedy of Errors* would be received from the start of showing. This was Shakespeare's introduction to the task of providing for the 'there and then' when launched on the 'here and now'. Yet not only was the Expository Inset, in the course of Shakespeare's career, understood to be shiftable to a position later than Act I, scene i, but it was perceived to be simply one kind of Inset, calling on only part of the poet's readiness to employ his narrative-descriptive art. Moreover, whenever that narrative-descriptive art was employed, it was clear that something must happen to the physically visible scene confronting the audience. The persons before that scene were frozen since the dramatic continuous *now* could not be advanced while another time and place were evoked or projected. The physical scene was endowed with a 'backing' or was occluded. The audience was to become bi-focal; beholding stilled figures within their physical sight, the audience imaginatively beheld persons, actions, places at a further reach, and what took place in that further reach set what they saw in perspective. In this way the 'profound' or the 'superficial', the 'dense' or the 'thin', of literary criticism have a more than mere metaphorical (or metaphysical), if still not entirely literal, application to Shakespeare on the stage.

The poet Shakespeare could not rest content in the practice of his narrative art and urge when it was limited to an expository motive. It was pure engineering, although the engineering could be beautifully developed as is shown by a comparison between the Expository Inset of *The Comedy of Errors* and that of *The Tempest*. Other possibilities of the Inset offered themselves. The most *obvious* possibility was indeed but a variant of the Expository. Embarked on the showing of the continuous *now* of a dramatic plot, there would be occasions when descriptive report would be more effective than demonstration. Or not simply more effective but essential, the only way out—and forward; or, more interesting, not essential, but preferable for a number of reasons more pleasing to the poet than the playwright, or equally pleasing to both. Practice in the Expository Inset, which was unavoidable, led to practice in the Interior Plot-required Inset which was, as often as not, a matter of choice. The plot might require this or that event in the sequence but there would be a choice of means—the means of drama and narrative. The re-union between Leontes and Perdita, in *The Winter's Tale*, Shakespeare chose to narrate. He could, of course, have shown: he did not necessarily choose as he did choose because narration is an inferior, or less affecting, mode. The descriptive means of narration *can* be more impressive, or equally impressive as the dramatic means, as Enobarbus has proved before—and on—his two audiences.

Which leads to the Voluntary. This type of Inset may have grown out of the Interior Plot-required as the Internal Plot-required had grown out of the Expository. It is less obviously functional, within the mechanics of a play, than either of the other, and in the main earlier, types, but perhaps precisely because it is less obviously functional, it is the Inset which demanded some of Shakespeare's fullest displays of energy. Unnecessary, inviting themselves to be cut from acting-versions, the Voluntaries nevertheless contain and control the central power and meanings of the plays in which they occur. When they occur they then reduce what is seen by the audience to proportion; until they occur something to—or behind—the play is wanting; after they have occurred they so reverberate that everything else the audience sees and hears is related to them. Webster was to learn from Shakespeare the power of the Voluntary Inset if he learnt nothing else; of course he did learn else.

No-one could make the sort of summary charge that Rahv brings against American literature (which nevertheless has its own exhilaration, stimulus and interest) against Shakespeare. To the collective memory, and to that he owed the Histories and the folk songs, he grafted his own memory; that is, his own experience both actual and literary. To the collective memory Shakespeare owed the folk, or seemingly folk, songs and, since these are supposed to antedate the characters of his play who sing or listen to them, they are obviously a kind of Inset. These songs had been sung before, they tell of other persons and places than are presented before the audience. Still, Shakespeare's own capital of memory grew.

But grew not in isolation from that of others nor in isolation from the evolution of the theatre—that box, arena or frame in which his poetry and drama originally happened. That box altered with the move from The Theatre to The Globe; and in 1608 or 1609 there was Blackfriars as an alternative or as an addition. From Globe to Blackfriars represented if not double purpose, or confusion, then (consider the valediction of Prospero) a trend of 'taste', however deplorable. Beaumont and Fletcher—brilliant and capable men—were active to prove the existence of this trend, and to exploit it.

Shakespeare had long past, in 'The Murder of Gonzago', shown his awareness of a kind of Inset that was framed beyond an innermost proscenium. *Pericles*, *Cymbeline*, *The Winter's Tale* and *The Tempest* were not bought cheap, or made cheap. They cost the price of all that had gone before. Given the chance of dramatizing memories, or of narrating memories that pressed against a *now*, a *now* which Prospero is not altogether helpless to direct, the poet-dramatist combined both his arts in a new way which still troubles.

Index

INDEX